The Identity Wheel

About The Author

Picture taken by Charlotte Nye – Unbound Photography 2025

Daniel James discovered his proven transformation methods after spending nearly three decades as what he calls "a prisoner of his own thoughts". Following his recovery from severe depression and destructive relationship patterns, he became a qualified NLP coach.

His systematic approach to identity-level change has helped hundreds of people overcome limiting beliefs through his flagship programme, Ascend. Daniel has spoken to over 12,000 students and delivered workshops for organisations including Audi, Nationwide, Distinct Recruitment and CDW. He hosts The Prime Life Project Podcast with over 350 episodes of practical mental health insights.

Daniel's mission emerged from his darkest moments: helping others recognise destructive patterns before they become entrenched, focusing on the crucial gap between knowing what to do and actually doing it.

To learn more about his Ascend coaching programme or speaking availability, visit www.theprimelifeproject.co.uk

Instagram - @Theprimelifeproject

Dedicated to everyone who believed in me when I couldn't believe in myself, and to my younger self who struggled in silence ... we did it.

The Identity Wheel

The Identity Wheel:

How to rewire your core beliefs and break free from self-sabotage

By Daniel James

The Identity Wheel

Copyright © 2025 Daniel James

All rights reserved. No part of this publication may be reproduced, stored in a retrieval system, or transmitted in any form or by any means, electronic, mechanical, photocopying, recording, or otherwise, without the prior written permission of the author.

First published 2025

ISBN: 978-1-9192790-0-8

The information in this book is based on the author's personal experience and research. It is not intended as a substitute for professional medical or psychological advice. Readers should consult with qualified professionals for issues relating to mental health, trauma or crisis situations.

Published by Prime Life Project Publishing

Contents

About The Author ii
Contents vii
Foreword by Peter Sage ix
Author's Note xiii
Introduction xv
Chapter 1: The Wheel: Understanding Personal Growth 1
Chapter 2: The Mind's Hidden Architecture 17
Chapter 3: Identity – The Core of Your Reality 37
Chapter 4: The Power of Thoughts and Beliefs 53
Chapter 5: Mastering Your Emotional Landscape 79
Chapter 6: Beyond Fear –Reclaiming Your Power 103
Chapter 7: Action – Bridging the Knowing-Doing Gap ... 127
Chapter 8: Breaking the Confirmation Loop 155
Chapter 9: Transforming Your Reality Through Mindset
.... 177
Chapter 10: Sustaining Your Transformation 201
Chapter 11: The Identity Wheel in Practice 225
Chapter 12: Transformation Stories 249
The 30-Day Identity Wheel Transformation Plan 271
    Week 1: See Your Current Pattern (Days 1–7) 271
    Week 2: Stop the Old Pattern (Days 8–14) 273
    Week 3: Install the New Pattern (Days 15–21) 275
    Week 4: Make It Stick (Days 22–30) 276
    Completion Criteria 278
    Emergency Support 279

The Next Step in Your Transformation Journey.................... 281
References.. 282
Acknowledgements 291

Foreword by Peter Sage

Every so often a book comes along that doesn't just inform, it transforms. *The Identity Wheel* is one of those rare works. It doesn't speak to who you think you are, it speaks directly to the deeper part of you that's always known there's more.

What Daniel has achieved here is something most authors only attempt. He hasn't simply written another self-help book filled with motivational soundbites or recycled platitudes about positive thinking. He's done something far more valuable. He's built a bridge between why you know what to do yet still don't do it, and the exact mechanisms required to finally change that.

Having spent decades teaching the psychology of transformation and the science of human behaviour, I can tell you this: real change doesn't happen through information. It happens through **identity evolution**. And that's precisely the heartbeat of this book.

Daniel's Identity Wheel isn't theory. It's a living model. It shows how our identity, thoughts, emotions, actions and results are not separate events but interconnected parts of a self-reinforcing cycle. Most people spin on that wheel for a lifetime, mistaking motion for progress. What Daniel offers is the way to step off the autopilot and take the wheel of your own life consciously.

The Identity Wheel

I particularly appreciate how he integrates ancient wisdom with modern neuroscience, merging ideas once confined to monasteries and meditation halls with cutting-edge insights from psychology and brain science. He reminds us that transformation is not about forcing the mind into submission but learning to work with its architecture, to reprogramme rather than resist.

The beauty of this work lies in its practicality. Daniel doesn't leave you in the clouds philosophising about potential. He hands you the tools to translate insight into embodiment. The exercises and reflections throughout the book turn theory into practice, guiding you step by step from awareness to action.

But perhaps what resonates most is Daniel's compassion. This isn't written from an ivory tower. It's written by someone who's wrestled with his own conditioning, fallen into his own cycles of self-sabotage, and done the inner work required to transcend them. That authenticity is what gives this book its power.

If you let it, *The Identity Wheel* will do far more than teach you how to think differently. It will invite you to become differently. It will help you see that you were never broken, only running an old programme designed for a life you've long outgrown. And it will show you how to install a new operating system built on truth, possibility and self-leadership.

In my own journey, I learned that true transformation doesn't come from striving harder but from shifting the identity at the root of everything. The greatest breakthroughs of my life came when I stopped forcing outcomes and instead focused on the deep shift in identity that aligned with my highest vision. It's not about overcoming obstacles, it's about letting go of the outdated versions of ourselves that are holding us back. This book is a blueprint for exactly that.

So, as you turn these pages, don't read them passively. Engage. Reflect. Question. Participate. Because what you hold in your hands isn't just a book, it's a mirror. One that reflects not the person you've been, but the person you're ready to become.

Welcome *to The Identity Wheel*. You're about to remember who you truly are. And, as I've learned from my own journey, when you step into that truth, the world will step aside to make room for you.

Peter Sage

Entrepreneur, Author, and Teacher of Consciousness & Human Potential.

The Identity Wheel

Author's Note

This book presents a powerful framework for personal transformation, but it's important to understand its limitations. The Identity Wheel has helped thousands of people, but it's not a substitute for professional therapy when dealing with trauma, severe mental health challenges, or crisis situations. If you're experiencing thoughts of self-harm or severe depression, please reach out to a qualified mental health professional or your doctor.

Personal transformation happens within broader social contexts. Whilst shifting your identity can create remarkable changes, some challenges may be rooted in systemic issues beyond individual mindset. This framework focuses on what's within your control whilst recognising that real barriers exist.

However, I believe deeply in the human capacity for growth. No matter where you find yourself today, meaningful change remains possible. Even in dark circumstances, small shifts in how we see ourselves can illuminate new pathways forward. This book offers practical tools that you can adapt to your unique circumstances. Change is rarely easy, but it's always possible when we understand how transformation actually works.

The Identity Wheel

Introduction

You know that moment when you do exactly the thing you promised yourself you wouldn't do? When you react the same way you always react, choose the same type of person who always hurts you, or sabotage yourself just when things are going well?

That moment isn't random. It isn't weakness. And it isn't something you can fix with more willpower or better intentions.

It's your life operating exactly as it was designed to by a system you built before you were old enough to know what you were building.

Maybe for you it's the promotion interview where your mouth goes dry and you downplay your achievements again. Or the relationship where you find yourself people-pleasing until you disappear again. Or the moment you scroll social media instead of working on the project that could change everything again.

These aren't character flaws. They're features of a perfectly functioning system that's been running your life from behind the scenes, creating the same patterns, the same limitations, the same frustrations, year after year.

What if I told you that the same invisible system that creates these patterns could be redirected to create entirely different results? That the very mechanism that keeps you stuck is the same one that could set you free?

The Identity Wheel

The problem isn't that you're broken. The problem is that you're running perfectly functioning software designed for the wrong life.

This book will show you how to recognise that software, understand how it operates, and consciously reprogramme it to create the life you actually want to live.

What This Book Solves:

- Why knowing what to do rarely leads to actually doing it
- Why traditional approaches to change often fail
- The hidden mechanics behind recurring life patterns
- How to bridge the gap between information and true transformation

What You'll Gain:

- A practical map of how your beliefs create your reality
- The precise intervention points to create lasting change
- An understanding of how to reprogramme your subconscious mind
- Specific techniques to transform limiting identities
- A complete framework that blends ancient wisdom with modern neuroscience

Who This Book Is For:

- If you've tried to change but keep falling back into old patterns
- If you feel like there's an invisible wall between you and the life you want

- If you're tired of reading self-help books without real change
- If you're ready to finally understand why you get stuck and how to break free

This isn't about positive thinking.

It isn't about forcing yourself to hustle harder.

It's about understanding the hidden architecture of your mind and learning to work with it instead of against it.

The Identity Wheel will show you how your identity, your thoughts, your emotions, your actions and your results are interconnected in a self-reinforcing loop. Once you understand this cycle, you can consciously interrupt it, reprogramme it and finally create lasting transformation from the inside out.

This book is a journey, not a lecture. I invite you to participate fully by journaling, reflecting and doing the exercises. Expect active transformation that requires your full participation.

The wheel of your mind is always turning. The only question is: **will you continue spinning in circles, or will you finally take the wheel and steer?**

The choice is yours. Let's begin.

The Identity Wheel

Chapter 1: The Wheel: Understanding Personal Growth

I didn't stumble across the Identity Wheel in a flash of enlightenment.

It wasn't one single moment. It was a slow realisation. One that started when I found myself sitting cross-legged on the floor of a small Buddhist centre, frustrated and restless.

I had come there searching for peace, but at first all I found was more noise inside my own head. Meditation felt impossible. Stillness felt unbearable. My mind raced with regrets, worries and self-judgement. Every part of me wanted to escape. But somewhere in the frustration, something began to shift.

The Identity Wheel

Through the ancient teachings shared there about the nature of suffering, the endless cycles of craving, action and consequence, I started to see a pattern emerge. It was like the faint outline of a map appearing on fogged glass.

For years, I had been collecting pieces: neuroscience, coaching, personal development theories. But I hadn't seen how they fit together. At the Buddhist centre, those scattered pieces started to click into place. Like finishing a jigsaw puzzle I didn't know I was solving.

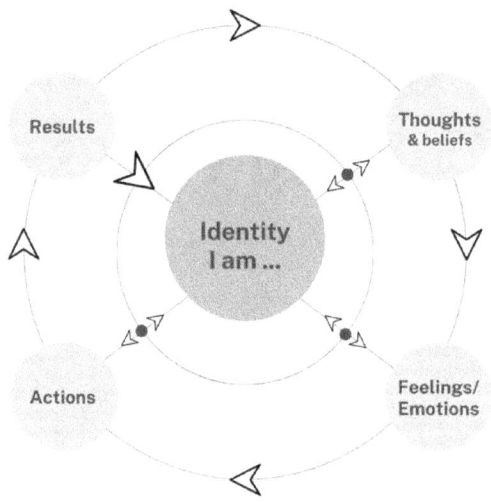

That's when I realised: the problem wasn't that I lacked discipline, or desire, or effort.

The problem was the hidden architecture of my mind itself, a self-reinforcing cycle of identity, thoughts, emotions, actions and results. A wheel.

A wheel that, once set in motion, could either trap me in suffering or set me free.

Chapter 1: The Wheel: Understanding Personal Growth

To truly understand this wheel and how it has shaped your reality up until now, we first need to look at the eternal dance between who you think you are, how you think and how you feel.

The Eternal Dance of Self

Imagine your life as a cosmic dance, where each step flows naturally into the next. At the centre of this dance lies your identity which is made up of the core beliefs about who you are; it's the voice you hear in the quiet moments when no one else is listening. These aren't our confident statements in business meetings or social gatherings. Instead, they're the raw, unfiltered "I am" statements that echo in our minds during moments of solitude: I am unworthy. I am unlovable. I am broken. I am resilient.

These identity statements form the foundation of our internal architecture, silently directing the flow of our thoughts like an invisible conductor. Each thought that crosses our mind must first pass through the filter of our identity, either reinforcing or challenging these core beliefs about who we are. Neuroscience research supports this, showing how our core beliefs create organisational patterns in the brain that filter incoming information [1].

What makes these identity statements so powerful is that they operate on a subconscious level. They're not the superficial self-assessments we share with friends or colleagues: "I am good at my job" or "I am a team player." Rather, they're the profound, often painful truths we mutter to and about ourselves when we're alone in the car, in the shower, or lying awake at night. They emerge most powerfully in moments of challenge or crisis: "I am so useless. I am such a failure. I am no good. I am rubbish. I am pathetic. I am unlovable."

I've hypothesised that many of us are walking around with what I call a "lie-dentity" which is a false self-image constructed from the harsh words and limiting beliefs others have impressed upon us. These aren't our true identity statements; they're lies we've been told about ourselves by people who didn't believe in us, didn't understand us or were projecting their own limitations.

Perhaps someone once told you, "You aren't good enough," and that prediction became a self-fulfilling prophecy. Each time you approached success, you found ways to sabotage it, unconsciously proving right those who doubted you.

This dance between our authentic identity and our lie-dentity creates a complex choreography that influences every aspect of our lives. This aligns with Carol Dweck's groundbreaking research on how our beliefs about ourselves powerfully shape our actions and outcomes [2]. The statements we hold about ourselves become the foundation upon which all other thoughts, beliefs and actions are built. When we carry a negative identity, it's like trying to build a magnificent castle on quicksand. No matter how beautiful the structure, the foundation cannot support it.

But here's the transformative truth: these identity statements, no matter how deeply ingrained, are not immutable facts. They are stories we've accepted about ourselves, often without questioning their validity or source. Just as a skilled dancer can learn new steps, we can learn to recognise these limiting identity statements for what they are – inherited beliefs and protective patterns that may have served us once but no longer reflect who we truly are or who we can become.

The first step in transforming our identity is simply becoming aware of these subconscious "I am" statements. Notice what you say to yourself when things go wrong. Pay attention to the automatic self-talk that emerges in moments of stress or challenge. These are not random thoughts, they're expressions of your current identity construction. By bringing them into consciousness, we begin the process of examining their truth and choosing whether they still serve us.

Remember, your identity is not a fixed star but a dynamic constellation of beliefs about yourself. While it may feel permanent and unchangeable, constellations actually shift over time as we change our vantage point and as the universe itself evolves. New stars can emerge, others can fade, and entirely new patterns can be discovered in the same sky. The question isn't whether these identity statements can change, it's whether you're ready to begin seeing new patterns and possibilities in your own constellation.

Here's what no one tells you: the strongest people aren't those who never doubt themselves. They're those who doubt themselves constantly but act anyway. Confidence isn't the absence of self-doubt – it's action in the presence of self-doubt.

The Thought-Belief Bridge

Our thoughts, persistent and recurring, eventually crystallise into beliefs. All beliefs are simply thoughts that we've kept on thinking and never stopped to challenge. You have beliefs about yourself that have no factual proof, yet you walk around believing them as facts. If they had facts, they would be facts and not beliefs. But you believe that you can't be successful, you believe you can only earn a certain amount of money, you believe you can't be happy, you believe, you believe, you believe. These beliefs act as the lens through which we interpret every experience, shaping our perception of what's possible and impossible in our lives.

The relationship between thoughts and beliefs is bilateral, creating a complex web of internal programming. Your thoughts will always lead to your feelings and emotions, but sometimes these feelings seem to arise spontaneously. This is because the predominant thoughts operating in your life often function at a subconscious level, they're part of your programming, running silently in the background of your mind. These are past thoughts you're holding onto that are causing your current feelings and emotions, even when you're not actively aware of them.

You have approximately 70,000 thoughts per day. About 95% of them are the same thoughts you had yesterday. You're not thinking your way to a new life; you're thinking your way to the same life, repeatedly.

But here's where the magic of the Identity Wheel reveals itself: these beliefs aren't fixed stars in our mental sky. They're more like clouds, capable of shifting and transforming when we learn to harness the wheel's momentum. By gaining awareness of our thought patterns and challenging our long-held beliefs, we can begin to reprogramme our internal dialogue and create new possibilities for ourselves.

Chapter 1: The Wheel: Understanding Personal Growth

The Emotional Landscape

As our thoughts and beliefs take root, they generate an emotional ecosystem within us—persistent weather patterns that characterise our daily experience rather than mere fleeting feelings. Recent neuroscience research has revealed that emotions aren't simply reactions to external events but are constructed by our brains based on past experiences and current context [3]. The wheel teaches us that emotions aren't random events happening to us; they're the natural result of our thoughts and beliefs. It's impossible to hold thoughts of abundance and feel scarcity simultaneously. You cannot entertain thoughts of self-worth and feel inadequate at the same time. Your emotional landscape is a direct reflection of your thought patterns.

Consider how a garden reflects the care it receives. Your emotional landscape mirrors the thoughts you've been planting and the beliefs you've been nurturing. A garden overgrown with fear-based thinking will produce anxiety and hesitation. A garden tended with self-compassion and possibility will yield confidence and resilience. The key is understanding that your feelings are like a barometer for your thoughts; if you're experiencing persistent negative emotions, it's a clear signal to examine the thoughts and beliefs generating them.

When you find yourself in emotional distress, remember that your feelings aren't arbitrary, they're giving you valuable information about your thought patterns. If you're feeling anxious, stressed or depressed, work backwards to uncover the thoughts creating these emotions. Even if you can't immediately identify the specific thoughts, know that they exist, operating beneath the surface of your conscious awareness. By acknowledging this connection between thoughts and emotions, you gain the power to change your emotional state by actively choosing different thoughts and challenging limiting beliefs.

Think of your emotional landscape as a feedback system, constantly providing information about the quality of your thoughts and beliefs. Just as a gardener wouldn't ignore wilting plants or invasive weeds, you shouldn't ignore persistent negative emotions. They're simply telling you it's time to tend to your mental garden, to examine the thoughts you're nurturing and the beliefs you're allowing to take root.

Action: The Physical Expression

Our emotions, in turn, drive our actions or, often, our inaction. This is where the wheel touches the ground of our physical reality. Someone believing "I am not creative" doesn't sign up for the art class. Someone feeling unworthy doesn't apply for the promotion. Our actions (or lack thereof) become the physical expression of our internal narrative.

Most of the time, we're not consciously choosing our actions, we're simply reacting based on our emotional state. When we feel anxious, we withdraw. When we feel unworthy, we self-sabotage. When we feel powerless, we don't even try. These reactions become so automatic that we rarely pause to question them. We might tell ourselves we're being "realistic" or "practical" but, in truth, we're simply acting out the script written by our identity, thoughts and beliefs.

The most insidious part of this process is how our actions, or lack of action, seem entirely logical given our emotional state. Of

Chapter 1: The Wheel: Understanding Personal Growth

course, you wouldn't apply for that dream job if you were feeling incompetent. Of course you wouldn't speak up in that meeting if you were feeling anxious. Of course you wouldn't start that business if you were feeling uncertain. Our actions feel like natural consequences of our emotions, but they're actually choices. Choices we're making from a place of unconscious programming rather than conscious intention.

The Confirmation Loop

Perhaps the most profound insight the Identity Wheel offers is understanding how the results we get or don't get can confirm our initial identity. When we act (or don't act) based on our emotions, we create results that often validate our original "I am" statements. It's a self-fulfilling prophecy, but one we can consciously redirect.

This confirmation loop is particularly powerful because it operates like a self-sealing system. If you believe you're not good enough, you'll feel anxious and inadequate, which leads to hesitant, half-hearted actions, or no action at all. These actions (or lack thereof) produce poor results, which then confirm your original belief: "See? I knew I wasn't good enough." The wheel completes another turn, and the cycle deepens.

But here's where understanding the wheel becomes transformative: this loop, though powerful, is not unbreakable. Every result we create is simply feedback and information we can use to adjust our course. Poor results don't prove our negative identity is "true"; they simply show us where our current beliefs and actions are leading us. By recognising this, we can begin to consciously interrupt the cycle at any point.

The confirmation loop isn't inherently negative; it's neutral, like any other natural process. Just as it can reinforce limiting beliefs, it can also strengthen empowering ones. When we understand this, we can begin to use the wheel's momentum to our advantage, consciously creating results that confirm more empowering identities and beliefs.

The key is remembering that while this loop might feel like destiny, it's actually a process we can influence. Every action we take, every result we create, is an opportunity to either reinforce our current identity or begin building a new one. The wheel will turn either way, the choice of direction is ours.

Breaking the Cycle: The Path to Transformation

The true power of understanding the Identity Wheel lies not in seeing how we're trapped, but in recognising the multiple points where we can intervene. Like a skilled DJ who can enter the beat at any point, we can step into this cycle and begin creating change wherever we find ourselves. This approach aligns with evidence-based psychological interventions that focus on disrupting unhelpful patterns at various points in the cognitive-emotional-behavioural cycle [4].

- We can question and reshape our identity statements
- We can challenge and reframe our thoughts
- We can cultivate different emotional responses
- We can take bold actions that defy our old patterns

Each point of intervention creates a ripple effect through the entire wheel, gradually shifting its momentum towards positive transformation.

Chapter 1: The Wheel: Understanding Personal Growth

Throughout the rest of this book, we'll explore how you can break the cycle through your mental muscles that may have grown weak and dusty from disuse. Like machines in an old factory, they need maintenance and care to begin working at full capacity again. You've had this power since birth, but perhaps you've never been taught how to use it effectively.

We'll discover how changing the way you look at things changes the things you look at. You'll learn to harness your willpower strategically, understanding it as a finite resource that needs to be directed wisely. We'll tap into the power of your imagination, not as mere daydreaming, but as a tool for creation and transformation.

This understanding of the wheel isn't just philosophy; it's a practical framework for creating lasting change. As we progress through this book, you'll learn to work with these natural processes rather than against them, creating transformation through awareness, understanding and consistent action.

Your identity isn't your destiny; it's your starting point.

Understanding the Identity Wheel offers more than insight – it offers hope. It shows us that we're not victims of fixed personality traits or unchangeable circumstances. We're active participants in a dynamic system that responds to conscious intervention.

Think of every limiting belief you've carried, every self-defeating thought pattern you've entertained, every emotional storm you've weathered; these aren't permanent fixtures of your personality but rather temporary patterns in a system you can learn to influence. Just as our negative patterns were created through repetition and reinforcement – new, empowering patterns can be established through conscious awareness and consistent action.

The wheel keeps turning, but we choose the direction. Every moment presents a new opportunity to step into a different part of the cycle and begin again. When you understand that your identity isn't fixed, that your thoughts aren't facts, that your emotions are feedback, and that your actions are choices, you gain access to profound personal power. Rather than abstract philosophy, you'll find a practical framework that creates immediate transformation.

As we move forward in this book, we'll explore each aspect of the wheel in greater detail. You'll learn specific techniques for interrupting negative patterns, tools for reshaping your identity and strategies for creating lasting change. We'll delve into the practical applications of your mental faculties and discover how to use them to their full potential.

For now, remember this: your journey of growth is just beginning. Let the Identity Wheel be your guide. You don't need to transform everything at once. Sometimes, shifting just one spoke of the wheel, questioning one identity statement, challenging one limiting belief, choosing one different emotional response or taking one bold action is enough to begin turning the entire system in a new direction.

The wheel is always in motion, constantly creating and reinforcing patterns in your life. The only question is: in which direction will you guide it? In the chapters that follow, you'll discover exactly how to take control of that direction and create the life you truly desire. The choice, as it has always been, is yours. Let's begin.

Chapter 1: The Wheel: Understanding Personal Growth

Chapter Summary

The Identity Wheel framework illustrates how identity, thoughts, emotions, actions and results form a self-perpetuating cycle.

Identity statements form the foundation of your internal architecture, directing the flow of thoughts and beliefs.

Thoughts and beliefs act as a bridge to your emotions, filtering your perception of what's possible.

Emotions serve as the natural result of your thoughts, creating your persistent emotional landscape.

Actions (or inaction) become the physical expression of your internal narrative, driven by your emotions.

Results you create confirm your initial identity in a self-fulfilling prophecy.

Breaking the cycle is possible by intervening at any point in the wheel, from identity to results.

Transformation occurs when you understand this cyclical process and consciously redirect its momentum.

Reflection Questions

1. When you reflect on areas of your life where you feel stuck, can you identify recurring patterns? What similarities do you notice across different situations?
2. How aware are you of the connection between your identity (how you see yourself) and the results you're experiencing in different areas of your life?
3. Think about a recent challenge you faced. Can you trace how your thoughts about this situation influenced your emotions, actions and, ultimately, the outcome?

Practical Exercises

1. Identity Exploration

- Take 10 minutes to write down all the "I am..." statements that come to mind when you think about yourself. Don't filter or judge, just capture everything that surfaces.
- Review your list and mark each statement as empowering (+) or limiting (-).
- Choose one limiting "I am" statement that feels significant. Where did this belief come from? What evidence supports or contradicts it?

2. Pattern Recognition

- Identify one area of your life where you feel stuck in a cycle.
- Map out the Identity Wheel for this situation:
    - Identity: What do you believe about yourself in this context?

Chapter 1: The Wheel: Understanding Personal Growth

- Thoughts: What thoughts arise from this identity?
- Emotions: What feelings do these thoughts generate?
- Actions: What behaviours result from these emotions?
- Results: What outcomes do these actions create?
- Confirmation: How do these results reinforce your original identity?

3. Wheel Awareness Practice

For the next week, set a daily reminder to pause and notice where you are in the Identity Wheel. Are you caught in a thought spiral? Experiencing strong emotions? Taking specific actions? Simply becoming aware of where you are in the cycle is the first step towards changing it.

The Identity Wheel

Chapter 2: The Mind's Hidden Architecture

In Chapter 1, we discovered how the Identity Wheel demonstrates the cyclical nature of our identity, thoughts, emotions, actions and results. But this raises an important question: Why does this wheel keep turning in the same direction?

To answer this, we need to understand the hidden machinery that powers these patterns – our mind!

Understanding the Blueprint

In this chapter, we'll discover:

- How your mind is structured and why this matters
- The relationship between your conscious and subconscious mind

- The five key characteristics that make your subconscious mind so powerful
- Why lasting change requires working with both levels of mind
- Understanding the Stick Person and the Power of Mental programmes

Have you ever wondered why, despite your best conscious efforts to change, you find yourself falling back into familiar patterns? Perhaps you've made New Year's resolutions with genuine intention, only to find yourself back in old habits by February. Or maybe you've attended motivational seminars, feeling incredibly inspired, only to have that inspiration fade within days.

If this sounds familiar, you're about to discover why and, more importantly, how to create lasting change.

In our previous chapter, we explored the Identity Wheel and how our identity creates a self-perpetuating cycle through our thoughts, emotions, actions and results.

Now, we're going to look behind the curtain and understand the machinery that powers this cycle. At the heart of this understanding lies a simple but profound model: the stick person.

The Architecture of Mind

Think of your mind as a modern home, with different levels that each serve a unique purpose. Your conscious mind is like the bright, open living space where daily life happens, where you make decisions, solve problems and interact with the world. It's where

Chapter 2: The Mind's Hidden Architecture

you're aware of your thoughts and actively choosing how to respond to life.

Beneath this active space lies something far more fundamental: your subconscious mind. Like the essential foundation and hidden systems of a house, it's largely unseen yet absolutely crucial. These lower levels aren't just practical spaces; they're the very bedrock upon which your entire mental house stands.

Here, in your subconscious, lie all your accumulated experiences, beliefs and patterns that shape your life. Just as a basement might hold generations of family belongings, your subconscious stores every significant experience, every repeated pattern and every deeply held belief you've ever absorbed.

Think about how a modern home depends entirely on these underlying systems. A problem with the wiring or plumbing will affect every room above, even if you can't see the issue from your living space. Similarly, the beliefs and mental programmes stored in your subconscious affect every aspect of your conscious life, often in ways you don't readily notice.

This house analogy helps us understand Dr Thurman Fleet's ingenious Stick Person model. Far from being just a simple drawing, this model captures a fundamental psychological truth through its elegant simplicity. Recent integrative approaches in neuroscience confirm this bidirectional relationship between our conscious thoughts and subconscious processing [5].

The Identity Wheel

Picture a circle, representing your entire mind, divided horizontally by a single line. Above this line sits your conscious mind, below it your subconscious, and connected at the bottom is a smaller circle representing your physical body.

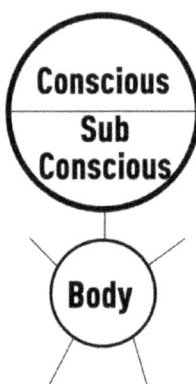

This simple diagram shows something remarkable about human consciousness. While we spend most of our waking hours engaged in conscious thought, planning, deciding and analysing, it's the subconscious mind that truly runs the show.

It's rather like a smart home: you might consciously flip a light switch, but it's the underlying operating system that actually controls how everything works.

The genius of Fleet's model lies in how it shows these parts working together. The horizontal line isn't a solid barrier but rather an interface between conscious and subconscious processes.

When you learn something new, for instance, it starts in the conscious mind. With repetition, it gradually sinks below that line

Chapter 2: The Mind's Hidden Architecture

into the subconscious where it becomes automatic, like when you first learned to drive compared to how naturally you do it now.

The moment you try to change everything is the moment you change nothing. Real transformation happens when you stop fighting your patterns and start redirecting them.

The connection to the body circle is equally important, showing how mental processes express themselves physically. Every thought above the line and every pattern below it eventually manifests through your physical form. This explains why confidence doesn't just change how you think, it changes how you stand, move and carry yourself.

Cell biologist Dr Bruce Lipton's groundbreaking research in epigenetics supports this mind-body connection. His work shows that our beliefs and perceptions, not just our genes, influence our biological functioning. Lipton's pioneering work in cell biology has shown how our perceptions, rather than genetic determinism, primarily control our biology [6].

"The moment you change your perception is the moment you rewrite the chemistry of your body," Lipton explains. This scientific validation of the mind's influence over the body reinforces the importance of addressing both our mental patterns and physical experiences in the transformation process.

Understanding this architecture explains why so many attempts at personal change fail.

Most of us try to create change at the conscious level only, like redecorating the living room while ignoring serious problems with the foundation. Real, lasting change requires us to work with both levels: using our conscious mind to direct change while addressing the deeper patterns in our subconscious that actually control our results.

The Stick Person and the Identity Wheel: A Powerful Partnership

Now that we understand the basic architecture of our mind through the Stick Person model, we can see how it powers the Identity Wheel we explored in Chapter 1. Think of the stick person as the engine room of your personal growth vehicle, while the Identity Wheel shows us the road it travels. When we overlay these two models, we begin to see why changing our results can be so challenging.

Our identity statements – the core "I am" beliefs we discussed in Chapter 1 – reside in the subconscious mind, below the line in our stick person model. These deep-seated beliefs then influence every thought that passes through our conscious mind above the line. This explains why the wheel keeps turning in the same direction – our subconscious identity is constantly filtering and directing our conscious thoughts to match its existing programming.

It's like having a sophisticated autopilot system that always wants to return to familiar territory. Understanding this relationship is crucial because it shows us where we need to intervene to create lasting change.

Simply trying to think positive thoughts (working above the line) isn't enough when your subconscious identity (below the line) remains unchanged. Real transformation requires us to work at

Chapter 2: The Mind's Hidden Architecture

both levels, using our conscious mind to direct new patterns while simultaneously reprogramming our subconscious beliefs.

Let's take a closer look at the conscious and subconscious mind.

The Conscious Mind: The Gatekeeper

Your conscious mind is the thinking mind, the educated mind, your rational architect of reality. It's where you actively engage with the world through your five senses: sight, sound, smell, taste and touch. Like a vigilant gatekeeper at an exclusive club, it's meant to evaluate and filter every piece of information before allowing it entry into your deeper mental territory.

This gatekeeper serves as your primary interface with the external world, with some research suggesting it's able to process roughly 40 bits of information per second. Here's where you:

- Analyse situations and make considered decisions
- Compare and contrast different options
- Form judgements based on available evidence
- Create new ideas and solutions
- Consciously choose your responses to situations

However, this gatekeeper isn't infallible, and this is crucial to understand.

During our formative years, particularly before the age of seven, this conscious filter hasn't fully developed its critical faculties. It's rather like having a security guard who's still training and allowing virtually everything to pass through unchallenged. This explains why childhood experiences have such a profound impact on our

23

later lives; they slip past our underdeveloped conscious filter and embed themselves directly into our subconscious programming.

The conscious mind accounts for only about 5–10% of our daily operations. This startling fact explains one of life's most frustrating paradoxes: why knowing what to do often isn't enough to create change. Simply put, our conscious mind is overruled by our subconscious patterns.

Think about it, how many times have you:

- Known you should exercise but found yourself on the settee?
- Understood you should save money but made an impulse purchase?
- Realised you should speak up at a meeting but remained silent?
- Meant to start a project early but put it off until the last minute?

This knowing-doing gap isn't a sign of weakness; it's evidence of the limited power of conscious thought alone. However, as you will learn throughout this book, it is through our ability to control the conscious mind that we can create the spark of change.

Your conscious mind might be the captain of the ship, but it's not the one actually moving the vessel through the water.

The Subconscious Mind: The Silent Engine Room

Your subconscious mind doesn't know the difference between what's real and what's vividly imagined. This is why you can feel genuinely afraid watching a horror film, even though you know it's not real. Your logical mind knows it's fiction, but your emotional mind treats the experience as real.

Beneath the surface of conscious awareness lies the true powerhouse of human behaviour: your subconscious mind. This is the emotional mind, the feeling mind, and it controls around 90–95% of our daily operations. Unlike your conscious mind, which processes 40 bits per second, neuroscience research suggests that your subconscious mind processes about 40 million bits per second – a million times more information.

The subconscious mind has several crucial characteristics that set it apart from conscious thought:

1. Acceptance Without Judgement

The subconscious mind operates like the most fertile garden soil you can imagine, it doesn't discriminate between the seeds of roses or weeds; it simply nurtures whatever is planted. This characteristic is both its greatest strength and potential weakness. Unlike your conscious mind, which can reason, debate and reject ideas, your subconscious mind operates on a simple principle: accept and grow.

Think about this process in action. Every thought you repeatedly think is like planting a seed in this fertile soil. When you constantly tell yourself "I'm not good at maths" your subconscious doesn't evaluate whether this is true or helpful – it simply accepts this as an instruction and begins creating evidence to support it.

This is why seemingly harmless thoughts, when repeated often enough, become deeply rooted beliefs that can shape your entire life experience.

This is particularly powerful when we consider how this acceptance mechanism worked in childhood. Perhaps a teacher once said you weren't creative, or a parent made an offhand comment about you being shy. These seeds, planted in your highly receptive young mind, might have grown into fully developed beliefs that still influence your behaviour today.

This is precisely what occurred when my year 11 history teacher stood me up in front of the class after I misbehaved and said, "You will never amount to anything." The humiliation I felt, compounded by my crush on the girl in front of me, caused that hurtful statement to take root in my subconscious. Looking back, I realise this belief was a major factor in causing me to sabotage much of my success.

2. Emotional Processing

While your conscious mind thinks in words and logic, your subconscious mind communicates through feelings and emotions. It's rather like having an ancient, sophisticated warning system installed in your body. When you walk into a room and feel inexplicably uncomfortable, or when you get a "gut feeling" about a situation, that's your subconscious mind processing countless subtle signals that your conscious mind hasn't even noticed.

Think about a time when you've met someone and had an immediate sense about them, only to later discover evidence that confirmed your initial impression. Your subconscious mind had already processed their tone of voice, micro-expressions, body language and countless other signals before your conscious mind could even begin its analysis

This emotional processing also explains why we can't simply "think" our way out of emotional reactions. You might consciously know that public speaking isn't life-threatening, but if your subconscious associates it with danger you'll experience real physical fear responses – sweating, increased heart rate, shaking – regardless of your rational thoughts. This evolutionary perspective on consciousness helps explain why our automatic responses often override our rational intentions.

3. Pattern Recognition and Execution

Your subconscious mind is the ultimate pattern recognition and execution system. It's constantly looking for recurring patterns in your experience and creating automated responses to handle them efficiently. This ability is what makes learning complex skills possible.

The driving example perfectly illustrates this. Remember your first driving lesson? Every single action required intense conscious focus:

- Check mirrors
- Signal
- Look over shoulder
- Press clutch
- Change gear
- Gradually release clutch while applying accelerator
- Maintain steering position
- Watch for hazards

Now, as an experienced driver, you can execute all these actions while holding a conversation about your day or planning your weekend. Your subconscious mind has recognised these patterns and created an automated programme to handle them, freeing your conscious mind for other tasks.

This same pattern recognition applies to everything from typing on a keyboard to emotional responses. If you've repeatedly responded to stress by becoming angry, your subconscious creates a pattern: stress = anger.

Dr Joe Dispenza explains this phenomenon through neuroscience: "Nerve cells that fire together, wire together." This principle, first articulated by psychologist Donald Hebb in 1949, remains a foundational concept in understanding how repeated patterns become physically encoded in neural circuitry [7]. When we repeatedly think the same thoughts or perform the same actions, we strengthen specific neural pathways until they become automatic. Dispenza's research combining neuroscience with meditation practices has shown how intentional thought can create measurable changes in brain function and even gene expression [8].

As he puts it, "We are not hardwired to be a certain way for the rest of our lives. We are hardwired to be able to change." This understanding gives us hope that, with conscious effort, we can create new patterns in our subconscious mind.

Understanding this is crucial because it means we can consciously create new patterns through consistent practice. More of that later.

Chapter 2: The Mind's Hidden Architecture

4. Literal Interpretation

The subconscious mind has no capacity for irony, sarcasm or jokes, it takes everything at face value. This characteristic makes it particularly susceptible to the language we use, both internally and externally. When you say things like "This always happens to me" or "I'm hopeless with money", your subconscious accepts these statements as literal commands and begins working to make them true.

This literal interpretation extends to imagery as well. When you vividly imagine something, your subconscious mind responds as if it were actually happening. This is why professional athletes can improve their performance through visualisation, because their subconscious mind processes the mental rehearsal as real practice.

Think about how often we use self-deprecating humour or make flippant comments about our abilities. While we consciously know we're joking, our subconscious mind is diligently recording these statements as truth and working to align our reality with them.

5. Perfect Memory

Your subconscious mind is like a vast digital archive that records everything (and I mean everything) you've ever experienced. Every sight, sound, smell, taste, touch, emotion and thought is stored away, even if you can't consciously recall it. This explains why certain smells can instantly transport you back to your grandmother's kitchen, or why a particular song can vividly recreate the emotions of your first love.

The Identity Wheel

Your subconscious mind, like a massive hard drive, stores every emotional imprint and behavioural pattern. Whether you frame it as cellular memory or karmic residue, the truth remains: your past shapes your present until you consciously step in to interrupt and rewire the pattern.

This perfect memory system operates independently of your conscious recall. You might not remember learning to walk, but your subconscious mind remembers every fall, every success and every encouragement that led to mastering this skill. This stored information becomes part of your operating system, influencing your current behaviour in ways you might not even realise.

Understanding this characteristic is particularly important when we consider trauma and limiting beliefs. Every negative experience, every harsh word, every failure is stored alongside the positive ones. These memories form the foundation of our beliefs about ourselves and the world, constantly influencing our present-moment choices and reactions.

Carl Jung, the renowned psychiatrist, described the subconscious as not merely a personal repository but as connected to what he called the "collective unconscious", a shared inheritance of experiences from our ancestors. "Until you make the unconscious conscious, it will direct your life and you will call it fate," Jung famously stated. His insight reminds us that bringing awareness to our subconscious patterns is the first step towards genuine freedom and choice.

The relationship between the conscious and subconscious minds is like that between a gardener and their garden. The conscious mind is the gardener who chooses what to plant, but the subconscious mind is the soil and the natural forces that actually grow the plants. You can consciously choose to plant tomatoes, but you can't consciously force them to grow; that's a subconscious process that follows natural laws.

Understanding this relationship is crucial because it explains why traditional approaches to personal change often fail. When we try to create change purely through conscious effort – through willpower and positive thinking alone – we're essentially trying to control the ocean's tides with a teaspoon.

Real, lasting change requires us to work with both levels of mind, using our conscious awareness to direct our attention while engaging the remarkable power of our subconscious mind to create lasting transformation.

Now that we understand the architecture of mind and how our conscious and subconscious aspects interact, we're ready to explore the cornerstone of personal transformation: our identity.

In the next chapter, we'll discover how your core identity forms within the subconscious mind, creating the foundation that either supports or undermines your efforts to change.

Looking Ahead

You now understand the architecture of the mind, its structure, its power, and its silent influence. But what exactly is being built atop that foundation?

The answer is identity. Your subconscious doesn't just process thoughts and memories; it constructs a sense of self. And that sense of self becomes the silent commander of your life.

The Identity Wheel

In the next chapter, we'll explore how your identity forms, how it operates below your awareness, and how transforming it becomes the most profound change you can make.

Chapter 2: The Mind's Hidden Architecture

Chapter Summary

The Stick Person model illustrates the distinct roles of the conscious and subconscious mind.

The conscious mind (above the line) processes roughly 40 bits of information per second and accounts for only 2–4% of daily operations.

The subconscious mind (below the line) processes about 40 million bits per second and controls 90–95% of our daily operations.

Five key characteristics of the subconscious mind: acceptance without judgement, emotional processing, pattern recognition, literal interpretation, and perfect memory.

The conscious-subconscious relationship explains why knowledge alone rarely creates change.

The Identity Wheel is powered by this mental architecture, with identity residing in the subconscious.

Real transformation requires working with both levels of mind rather than conscious effort alone.

Understanding this architecture provides the foundation for effective personal change.

REFLECTION QUESTIONS

1. How would you describe the relationship between your conscious and subconscious mind based on what you've learned?
2. When have you experienced the "knowing-doing gap" most strongly in your life? What might be happening beneath the surface?
3. Which of the five characteristics of the subconscious mind (acceptance without judgement, emotional processing, pattern recognition, literal interpretation, perfect memory) do you find most relevant to your personal challenges?

PRACTICAL EXERCISES

1. Conscious-Subconscious Dialogue

- Create two columns on a page: "Conscious Mind" and "Subconscious Mind"
- Choose a goal you've struggled to achieve
- In the first column, write what your conscious mind says about this goal
- In the second column, write what your subconscious might be saying (the resistance, fears or contradictory beliefs)
- Look for disconnects between the two perspectives

2. Mental Architecture Observation

- For one day, keep a simple tally of how often you notice:
    - Your conscious mind making a decision

Chapter 2: The Mind's Hidden Architecture

- - Your subconscious automatically handling a situation
  - A conflict between what you consciously want and what automatically happens
- At the end of the day, reflect: What percentage of your activities were conscious versus automatic?

3. Subconscious Pattern Detection

- Identify three habitual behaviours you perform without thinking
- For each one, try to trace back:
  - When and how did you learn this behaviour?
  - What triggered it to become automatic?
  - What purpose does it serve for you?
- Choose one habit you'd like to modify and write down what makes it challenging to change

The Identity Wheel

Chapter 3: Identity – The Core of Your Reality

In Chapters 1 and 2, we explored the Identity Wheel and the architecture of the mind that powers this transformative cycle. Now let's turn our attention to the cornerstone of personal transformation: your identity.

Your identity – those core beliefs about who you are – sits at the top of the Identity Wheel, silently orchestrating every aspect of your life experience. Like a conductor who never takes a bow, your identity directs the symphony of your thoughts, emotions, actions and, ultimately, your results. Understanding and reprogramming this central force is perhaps the most powerful transformation you can undertake. Research in narrative psychology shows how these identity stories become the organising principles of our entire personality [9].

The Power of "I Am"

The two most powerful words in the English language might well be "I am". These simple words shape how you see yourself and your possibilities. Whatever follows "I am" becomes more than a description; it becomes an instruction to your mind about who you are.

When you say, "I am intelligent" or "I am not good with money", you're programming your subconscious with directions that influence what opportunities you notice, what actions feel natural, and ultimately what results you achieve.

As Jesus states in the Bible, "I am the door" (John 10:9). This metaphor reveals a profound truth: your self-concept is the gateway through which all your experiences must pass. In the Quran, Allah's creative power is expressed through "Kun fayakun" (Be, and it is) demonstrating how declaration brings reality into existence.

Similarly, in the Bhagavad Gita (10:8), Krishna declares, "I am the source of all spiritual and material worlds. Everything emanates from me; and from me, all that is, has its origin," emphasising the creative power of the "I am" statement. The Mandukya Upanishad with Adi Shankara's commentaries teaches that Turiya, the fourth state of consciousness, represents the ultimate unqualified "I am", pure consciousness beyond all limitations. These wisdom traditions all point to the same truth: your "I am" declarations hold immense creative power. If you want confidence but keep telling yourself "I am shy", you create a contradiction that your mind must resolve, and it will typically default to your established subconscious identity.

These "I am" statements aren't just the positive things we say in public. They're often the unspoken beliefs that surface during difficult moments. They're what you whisper to yourself when you

Chapter 3: Identity – The Core of Your Reality

fail, face challenges or sit alone with your thoughts. These quiet declarations ultimately shape your reality more than what you say publicly.

Think about what you automatically say to yourself when things go wrong. Do you think, "I always mess this up" or "I'm useless at this"? These seemingly harmless reactions are actually powerful identity statements that your subconscious mind is recording and reinforcing.

Your identity statements work like filters, determining what information gets through to you and how you interpret it. If your identity includes "I am bad with technology", you'll likely notice every mistake you make with computers while overlooking your successes. The same experiences could happen to someone with the identity "I am great with technology", yet they would interpret them completely differently.

What makes these identity statements so influential is that they operate below your conscious awareness. They're not the surface-level assessments you share with others like, "I'm pretty good at my job" or "I'm working on being more patient". Instead, they're the deep-seated beliefs that form the foundation of how you see yourself in relation to the world. Research distinguishes between core identity and the multiple self-concepts we develop in response to environmental demands and social expectations [10].

Every time you say "I am..." you're making a declaration about your place in the universe. You're telling your mind, "This is who I am, so create more evidence of this." Your subconscious then diligently works to prove you right, regardless of whether the identity serves your growth or limits it.

You've probably spent more time choosing what to watch on Netflix than choosing who you believe yourself to be. Yet one decision lasts two hours, and the other lasts a lifetime.

The "Lie-dentity" vs. Your True Self

Many of us are walking around with what I call a "lie-dentity" which is a false self-image constructed from the harsh words and limiting beliefs others have impressed upon us. These aren't our true identity statements; they're lies we've been told about ourselves by people who didn't believe in us, didn't understand us, or were projecting their own limitations.

LIE-DENTITY	TRUE IDENTITY
The false self built from inherited limitations and others' projections	The authentic self rooted in truth, possibility, and self-worth
• I am not enough	• I am enough
• I am unworthy	• I am worthy
• I am broken	• I am whole
• I am a failure	• I am capable
• I am unlovable	• I am lovable
• I am not smart enough	• I am resilient
• I don't belong	• I am intelligent
• I am bad with money	• I am abundant
• I can't change	• I can change
• I always mess things up	• I am resourceful
• I am a burden	• I am strong

Perhaps you had a teacher who told you that you'd never amount to anything (as happened to me with my Year 11 history teacher). Maybe a parent constantly compared you unfavourably to a sibling. Or perhaps an early romantic partner criticised aspects of your appearance that you now view as fundamental flaws.

Chapter 3: Identity – The Core of Your Reality

These external messages don't just bounce off us – they can penetrate deeply, especially when we're young or vulnerable. Over time, we might come to believe these messages are actually truths about who we are, rather than someone else's limited perception or projection.

What makes identifying these "lie identities" so challenging is that we've wrapped our sense of self around them for protection. We've built elaborate systems of behaviour to adapt to these perceived limitations. If you believe "I am not smart enough", you might avoid intellectual challenges, prepare excessively for tests or develop compensating skills, all of which can be successful adaptations that seem to validate the original limiting belief.

This transformation from limiting to empowering identity is beautifully illustrated by Priya's journey

Priya's hands trembled as she stared at the promotion application on her computer screen. Marketing Director, the role she'd dreamed about for three years. But instead of excitement, she felt that familiar wave of nausea wash over her.

"I'm not smart enough for this," she whispered to herself, the words as automatic as breathing. This belief had roots that ran deep: years of being compared to her brother Arjun, the family's "golden child" who absorbed information effortlessly while she struggled through every assignment. "Arjun just gets things the first time," her father would say when she asked for help. "You just need to work harder, beta. Not everyone can be naturally gifted."

Despite graduating with honours (achieved through countless all-nighters), Priya attributed her success to "just working harder, not being smarter". In meetings, she'd have brilliant insights but keep them silent, certain that speaking up would expose her as the fraud she believed herself to be. When colleagues praised her record-breaking campaigns, she'd deflect: "I just spent ages on it. Anyone could have done the same."

The promotion deadline was tomorrow. Then her phone buzzed, a text from her mother: "So proud of how well you're doing, Priya." The words hit her differently this time. Proud of her, the "slow" one who supposedly lacked Arjun's natural gifts. For the first time, a crack appeared in her lifelong belief.

She opened a new document and began listing every achievement, every creative solution, every successful project. The evidence was overwhelming. Within minutes, she realised she hadn't succeeded despite lacking intelligence, she'd succeeded because she was genuinely brilliant. Three months later, when Priya received the promotion, she understood: she hadn't become smarter. She'd simply stopped believing the lie that she was stupid.

Priya's transformation illustrates the heart of identity work: recognising that our most limiting beliefs are often inherited stories rather than personal truths. The challenge is that these false identities persist because our adaptations to them actually work, creating reinforcing loops that make limiting beliefs seem increasingly valid over time.

Understanding how these inherited stories take root in the first place, and why they feel so convincingly true, requires us to examine the critical period when our core identity first forms

Chapter 3: Identity – The Core of Your Reality

The Origins of Your Core Identity

To understand how your identity formed, let's return to the Stick Person model we explored in Chapter 2. Remember that from ages zero to seven, children don't have fully developed critical faculties of the conscious mind. During this period, "the gatekeeper" is essentially off-duty, allowing all manner of programming to enter directly into the subconscious.

Your earliest identity statements formed during this crucial window. Developmental psychologists have long recognised these early years as critical for identity formation, with these early beliefs often persisting throughout the life cycle [11]. If you were consistently told you were clever, brave or capable, these empowering beliefs likely established themselves as your core identity. Conversely, if you received messages that you were troublesome, slow or unworthy, these limiting beliefs will have found their way into your identity structure with equal ease.

This early programming is particularly powerful because it occurs before we develop the ability to question or evaluate what we're told. As young children, we accept the definitions others give us as absolute truths. If a parent repeatedly says, "You're so careless," a child doesn't think, "Well, that's just Dad's opinion when he's stressed." Instead, the child simply accepts: "I am careless." This becomes part of their identity foundation.

Beyond direct statements, your identity was also shaped by:

Environmental Influences: The overall atmosphere of your home. Was it loving and supportive or critical and demanding? Did your family focus on abundance or scarcity? Were mistakes treated as learning opportunities or failures? These environmental factors shape your sense of what's normal and possible.

Observed Behaviours: Children learn not just from what they're told, but from what they witness. If you observed your parents or caregivers struggling with money, you might have formed an identity statement around financial limitation without anyone explicitly telling you that money is hard to come by.

Emotional Associations: If you received attention when you achieved academically but were overlooked when you displayed creativity, you might have formed an identity statement around academic achievement being your only path to recognition and love. The emotional imprinting that occurs during identity formation creates powerful neural networks that link our sense of self with specific emotional states [12].

As we grow older, these core identity statements become the filter through which we interpret all new experiences. They form our mental programmes that have almost exclusive control over our habitual behaviour. These mental programmes create the prism through which we view and make sense of the world around us.

Identity and Energetic Vibration

When we delve deeper into understanding identity, we encounter a fundamental truth shared by both ancient traditions and modern science: we are energetic and emotional beings. Everything in the universe is in motion, including our thoughts and internal states. Neuroscience shows that different emotional patterns influence brain chemistry and autonomic nervous system activity, which in turn affect decision-making, perception and physical behaviour

Chapter 3: Identity – The Core of Your Reality

[8]. What spiritual traditions have long described as "vibration" or "frequency", modern science might describe as emotional states, neural patterns or physiological coherence.

Your identity, especially the core "I am" statements you believe, generates a consistent emotional baseline. That baseline becomes your internal frequency. A belief like "I am unworthy" creates a very different neurological and emotional reality to "I am enough". These patterns shape what you notice, how you feel and what you attract or repel, both socially and energetically [10].

Whether you think of this in terms of energetic alignment or cognitive bias, the effect is the same: we become magnets for experiences that match our internal state. The subconscious mind is constantly scanning for confirmation of our self-image; spiritually, we might say "we attract it" but, psychologically, we're simply reinforcing what we already believe to be true.

This explains why someone with a core identity of "I am unworthy" might repeatedly attract relationships where they're undervalued, despite consciously desiring respect. Their conscious desires are broadcasting at one frequency, but their core identity is broadcasting a much stronger signal at a different frequency.

The universe responds not to what you want, but to who you are, to the energetic signature of your identity. This weaves practical psychology together with energetic principles. When you believe certain things about yourself, you notice and gravitate towards evidence that confirms these beliefs while overlooking evidence that contradicts them.

The Identity Wheel

When you shift your identity, you shift your energetic frequency. This isn't merely poetic; it's a practical application of universal laws. As Tesla noted, "If you want to find the secrets of the universe, think in terms of energy, frequency, and vibration." Your identity is your fundamental energetic blueprint, and when you change it you change what resonates with you.

The Ripple Effect of Identity Shifts

When you change your identity (your core "I am" statements) the effects ripple through the entire Identity Wheel. Let's follow this transformation through each element of the wheel:

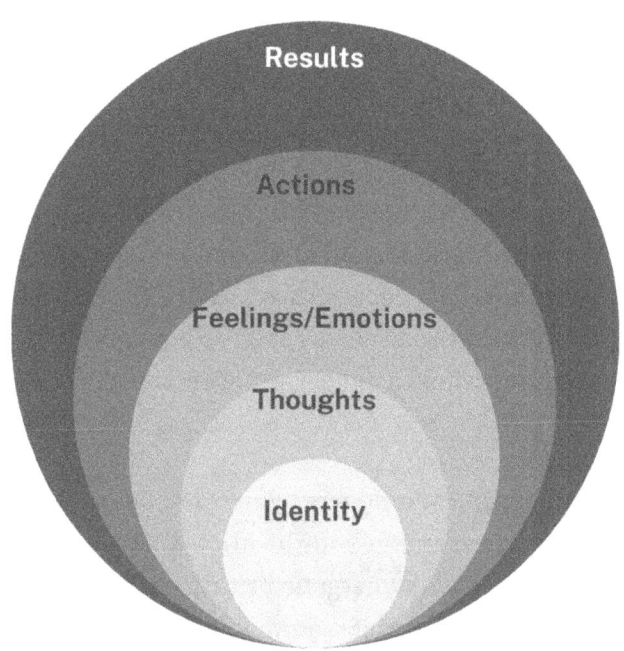

Chapter 3: Identity – The Core of Your Reality

Identity → Thoughts: When you shift from "I am financially limited" to "I am naturally abundant", your thoughts automatically begin to focus on opportunities and abundance rather than scarcity and limitation. You start thinking, "How can I increase my wealth?" instead of "How can I avoid running out of money?"[5].

Thoughts → Feelings: These new abundance-focused thoughts generate feelings of confidence, possibility and enthusiasm rather than anxiety, fear and resignation. You feel empowered rather than constrained when facing financial decisions.

Feelings → Actions: Feeling confident and abundant leads to: Bold actions, investing, learning about wealth creation and networking with successful people, rather than cautious, protective behaviours. You might ask for a raise, start a side business or make that investment you've been considering.

Actions → Results: These new actions inevitably create different results: Increased income streams, investment returns, valuable connections. Your financial situation begins to transform as a direct result of your transformed identity.

Results → Identity Confirmation: These improved results confirm and strengthen your new identity as someone who is naturally abundant, creating a positive spiral. "See? I truly am financially savvy," becomes your new truth, reinforced by tangible evidence.

This is the power of identity transformation; it changes everything downstream in your life experience. The challenge, of course, is that changing something as fundamental as identity rarely feels comfortable or natural at first. Your old identity, even if limiting, is familiar territory. Your subconscious mind values consistency and safety above all else, and it will work to maintain the status quo, even when the status quo isn't serving your highest good.

Research on self-efficacy, which is our belief in our ability to succeed in specific situations, shows how these beliefs determine what challenges we approach and how much effort we invest [13]. When your identity shifts to include stronger self-efficacy beliefs, your willingness to take on challenges and persist through difficulties naturally increases.

The Promise of Identity Transformation

As we conclude this chapter on identity, the core of your reality, let's reflect on what becomes possible when you consciously reshape your fundamental "I am" statements.

When you transform your identity, you don't just change what you do or what you have, you change who you are at the foundational level. This transformation ripples through every aspect of your life, from your closest relationships to your work, your health and your sense of purpose.

The most profound shift that occurs is that you no longer need to force yourself to take actions that align with your goals. These actions begin to feel natural because they're aligned with who you now are. The struggle between wanting and doing diminishes as your identity, thoughts, feelings and actions come into harmony.

Think of every limiting belief you've carried, every self-defeating thought pattern you've entertained, every emotional storm you've weathered – these aren't permanent fixtures of your personality

Chapter 3: Identity – The Core of Your Reality

but rather temporary patterns in a system you can learn to influence. Just as your negative patterns were created through repetition and reinforcement, new, empowering patterns can be established through conscious awareness and consistent action.

In the chapters that follow, we'll build on this foundation of identity as we explore the remaining elements of the Identity Wheel in greater detail. You'll learn specific techniques for interrupting negative patterns, tools for reshaping each aspect of the wheel and strategies for creating lasting change.

For now, remember this: your journey of transformation begins with those two simple but profound words: "I am". Choose them wisely, for they are quite literally creating your reality.

Chapter Summary

"I am" statements are the most powerful words shaping your sense of self and possibilities.

The "lie-dentity" comprises false self-images constructed from others' limiting perspectives.

Core identity forms primarily between ages 0 and 7 when the conscious mind's critical faculties aren't fully developed.

Identity has vibrational energy that attracts matching experiences, people and circumstances.

Identity shifts create ripple effects through thoughts, feelings, actions and results.

Transforming identity requires questioning limiting statements and creating new, empowering ones.

Evidence collection helps build new identity statements that feel authentic and aligned.

Wholeness emerges when you shed limiting beliefs and embrace your authentic capabilities.

Chapter 3: Identity – The Core of Your Reality

REFLECTION QUESTIONS

1. What core "I am" statements have shaped your life most significantly? Can you identify which ones might be "lie-dentities" rather than authentic truths?
2. How has your identity created a self-fulfilling prophecy in an important area of your life?
3. If you were to embrace your authentic identity without limitations, what might be possible for you?

PRACTICAL EXERCISES

1. Identity Archaeology

- Reflect on your childhood and early influences
- Who were the most influential figures in your formative years?
- What messages did you receive about who you are and what you're capable of?
- Which of these messages still influence your identity today?
- Note: This exercise offers just a taste of the deeper identity work available in the Ascend programme

2. Identity Evidence Collection

- Select one limiting identity statement you're holding
- Create two columns: "Evidence For" and "Evidence Against"
- List all the experiences that have reinforced this identity
- Challenge yourself to find at least three pieces of evidence that contradict this belief

- Consider: Which evidence are you giving more weight to, and why?

3. Future Identity Visioning

- Write a brief description of who you would be if you weren't limited by your current identity
- How would this person think, feel and act differently from how you do now?
- Identify one small way you could embody this future identity today
- Try acting "as if" you already embody this identity for 30 minutes and note the changes you experience

Chapter 4: The Power of Thoughts and Beliefs

In the previous chapters, we've explored how the Identity Wheel demonstrates the cyclical nature of our identity, thoughts, emotions, actions and results. We've examined the architecture of the mind that powers this wheel and examined how your core identity shapes your reality. Now, we turn our attention to the second element of the wheel: your thoughts and beliefs, the powerful forces that bridge your identity to your emotions and actions.

The Thought-Belief Connection

Your thoughts are the mental activity that occurs in response to your identity statements. Think of your identity as the soil and your thoughts as the seeds that are planted within it. The soil's quality determines which seeds will flourish and which will struggle to take root. If your core identity includes "I am creative", thoughts about innovative possibilities will naturally flourish. If, however, your identity includes "I am not good with numbers", thoughts of anxiety and inadequacy will sprout whenever mathematical challenges arise. This maths example is something I still have to be aware of to this day.

This connection is bilateral, creating a complex web of internal programming that perpetuates itself. This connection between thoughts and emotional responses forms the foundation of cognitive therapy, one of the most proven methods to improve psychological well-being [14]. The thoughts that flow from your identity eventually crystallise into beliefs which are those convictions that govern your perception of reality. As Earl Nightingale wisely observed in 'The Strangest Secret' , "We become what we think about most of the time." This simple wisdom lies at the heart of personal transformation.

All beliefs are simply thoughts that you've kept on thinking without challenge or interruption. They become the mental lenses through which you interpret every experience, shaping your perception of what's possible and impossible in your life. You have beliefs that feel like facts, even when there's no objective proof, and they quietly govern your behaviour until you bring them into the light.

Consider how many of your beliefs about yourself would crumble under proper scrutiny. You believe you can't be successful, you believe you can only earn a certain amount of money, you believe you can't be happy, you believe, you believe, you believe. If these were facts, they would be facts and not beliefs. But you've thought these thoughts so consistently that they've hardened into beliefs that feel unquestionable.

Chapter 4: The Power of Thoughts and Beliefs

This automatic nature of our thinking patterns aligns with what Nobel Prize-winning psychologist Daniel Kahneman describes in his groundbreaking research on how our minds work. Kahneman identified two distinct systems of thinking: System 1, which operates fast and intuitively without conscious effort, and System 2, which is slower, more deliberate, and requires conscious mental energy. The vast majority of our daily thoughts, including our beliefs about ourselves operate through System 1, running automatically in the background without our conscious awareness or questioning [15].

This explains why limiting beliefs feel so "true" and why they're so difficult to change, because they've become part of our automatic mental programming, operating below the threshold of conscious examination.

The Vibrational Nature of Thoughts

To truly understand the power of thoughts, we must recognise their energetic nature. Drawing from the wisdom of Nikola Tesla, who said, "If you want to find the secrets of the universe, think in terms of energy, frequency, and vibration," we can understand that thoughts are not merely abstract concepts but energetic frequencies that resonate throughout your entire being.

Your thoughts vibrate at different frequencies depending on their nature. Thoughts of gratitude, possibility and joy vibrate at high frequencies, while thoughts of fear, scarcity and resentment vibrate at lower frequencies. These vibrations don't remain isolated in your mind; they ripple outward, affecting your body, your emotions and, ultimately, the reality you experience. Recent neuroscientific research has shown how gratitude practices can substantially alter brain function and improve both psychological and physiological health markers [16].

Tom's alarm buzzes at 5:30 AM, and before his feet touch the floor, he's already begun his daily ritual. Sitting on the edge of his bed, hand on heart, he whispers: "Thank you for this breath, for this body that serves me, for another day to guide others towards peace." As he moves through his morning routine, gratitude flows like water, the appreciation for hot coffee, for sunlight streaming through his window, even for the early morning traffic that gives him moments of stillness.

When Tom arrives at the yoga studio, something remarkable happens before he even speaks. New students approach him with comments like, "There's something so calming about your energy" or "I felt my anxiety ease just standing near you". His classes consistently have waiting lists, not because of his advanced poses but because of the frequency he emanates.

Meanwhile, across town, Marcus starts each day with his mental catalogue of potential disasters. The difficult student who might disrupt class. The studio owner making pointed comments about attendance numbers. The scathing online review calling his teaching "cold and unwelcoming". Despite superior technical skills and more certifications than Tom, Marcus's classes feel tense and urgent. Students leave feeling more anxious than when they arrived.

The contrast is stark: Marcus demonstrates advanced poses flawlessly, but his energy field, which is generated by chronic worry and self-protection, creates an invisible barrier. Students sense something "off" and rarely return, though they can't

Chapter 4: The Power of Thoughts and Beliefs

articulate why. His mental rehearsal of worst-case scenarios manifests as the very rejection he fears.

After two years, Tom has transformed lives and built a thriving practice, while Marcus struggles to maintain basic enrolment. They teach the same poses in the same space but create entirely different realities through the vibrational frequency of their thoughts.

Think about how you can sense someone's mood on entering a room, even before they speak. What you're picking up is the vibrational frequency of their thoughts and emotions. This works both ways, others can sense your energetic state just as you sense theirs. This is why people often refer to "good vibes" or "bad vibes", they're intuitively sensing the vibrational frequency of your thought patterns.

When you consistently think thoughts that align with your desired reality, you begin to vibrate at the frequency of that reality. Like a tuning fork that causes another of the same frequency to vibrate in harmony, your thoughts attract experiences, opportunities and circumstances that match their vibration. This is not mystical thinking; it's practical psychology combined with energetic principles.

The Evolution from Thoughts to Beliefs

Understanding how thoughts evolve into beliefs is crucial for personal transformation. This process typically unfolds in predictable stages:

The Identity Wheel

1. **Initial Exposure**: You encounter a thought, either from external sources or your own mind.
2. **Repetition**: Through repetition, the thought gains familiarity and strength. Each time you think it, neural pathways in your brain strengthen.
3. **Emotional Attachment**: When emotions connect with thoughts, they accelerate belief formation. Emotionally charged thoughts become beliefs much faster than neutral ones.
4. **Evidence Gathering**: Your subconscious mind begins collecting evidence that confirms the emerging belief, often overlooking contradictory evidence.
5. **Belief Crystallisation**: Eventually, the thought becomes so ingrained that it transitions into a belief – a mental construct you no longer question but accept as truth.
6. **Identity Integration**: The strongest beliefs become integrated into your identity, transforming from "I believe" to "I am".

Chapter 4: The Power of Thoughts and Beliefs

01 — Initial Thought
A thought appears from external or internal sources

02 — Repetition
The thought is rehearsed in the constious mind or speech

03 — Emotional Charge
Emotions connect with the thought, accelerating belief formation

04 — Evidence Gathering
Attention filters for proof and contradictions are ignored

05 — Belief Crystallisation
The thought becomes an unquestioned belief

06 — Identity Integration
It becomes 'who I am', shaping choices and behaviour

This process can work either for you or against you, depending on the thoughts you consistently entertain. The Identity Wheel shows us that our thoughts and beliefs are not fixed but can be consciously directed. By understanding this evolutionary process, you gain the power to intervene at any stage and redirect your belief formation towards empowering rather than limiting constructs.

Challenging and Reframing Limiting Beliefs

The first step in transforming limiting beliefs is identifying them. These are often disguised as "truths" about yourself or the world that you've never properly questioned. They typically contain absolute language like "always", "never", "everyone" or "no one". Examples include "I'll never be good at public speaking", "I always mess up important opportunities" or "Everyone in my family struggles financially".

Once identified, these beliefs can be challenged through a systematic process:

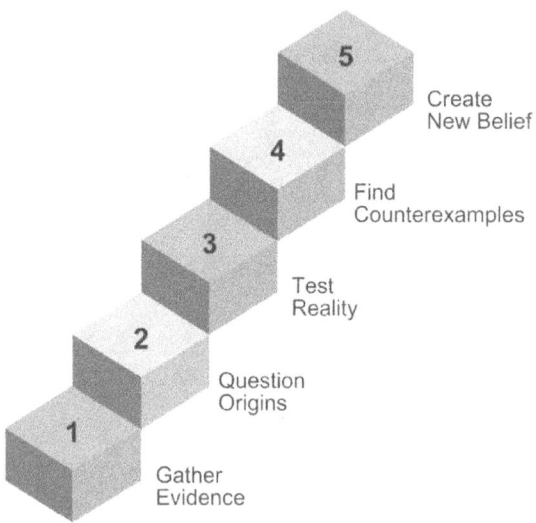

1. **Gather Evidence**: Look for evidence that contradicts your limiting belief. If you believe you "always fail", list instances where you've succeeded, no matter how small.
2. **Question Origins**: Ask yourself, "Where did this belief come from? Who taught me this? Does the source have credibility in this area?"
3. **Test Reality**: Put your belief to the test in small, low-risk situations. If you believe you're "not creative" try a simple

creative activity and observe the results without judgement.
4. **Find Counterexamples**: Look for people who disprove your belief. If you believe "no one from my background can succeed", find examples of those who have.
5. **Create a New Belief**: Craft an alternative belief that serves you better. Make it realistic, positive and in the present tense.

Here's a hypothetical example that shows how this process might work in a different context. Imagine someone named Emma, a project manager in a tech firm who has always defined herself as "analytical, not creative". This belief originated in her secondary school art class, where a teacher had commented that her work was "technically correct but lacks imagination".

As an adult, Emma struggles with leading brainstorming sessions and developing innovative solutions for her team. She often defers to others, prefacing her own ideas with "I'm not creative, but..."

If Emma were to apply the five-step process, she might first gather evidence that contradicts her belief. Though she doesn't consider herself "creative" in the traditional sense, she has successfully reorganised her department's workflow, developed unique solutions to logistical problems and even designed an effective home office space during the pandemic.

Next, she might question the origin of this belief, realising that a single art teacher's comment about one specific type of creativity had somehow expanded to define her entire creative capacity.

Emma could then test her belief in low-risk situations by joining an online design thinking course and finding that she actually excels at creative problem-solving when it's approached systematically. She might also participate in a team hackathon where her "non-artistic" perspective leads to a novel solution that is ultimately implemented.

She would find counterexamples by researching successful innovators who didn't fit the stereotype of "artistic creatives" but who transformed their industries through different forms of creativity.

Finally, Emma might craft a new belief: "I have a unique form of systematic creativity that allows me to see innovative solutions others might miss." This new belief would empower her to lead brainstorming sessions with confidence, potentially resulting in her team generating many more implementable ideas.

What makes this transformation particularly powerful is recognising that she doesn't need to become "artistic" to be creative, she simply needed to embrace her own distinct form of creativity, which had been there all along. Research on mindfulness shows that becoming aware of our automatic categorisations and assumptions creates cognitive flexibility that allows for new possibilities [17].

The Law of Vibration and Thought Frequency

When we dive deeper into understanding the power of thoughts, we encounter the Law of Vibration, which is a universal principle stating that everything in the universe moves and vibrates at

Chapter 4: The Power of Thoughts and Beliefs

different rates. Quantum physics reveals that all matter exists in a constant state of vibration, including our bodies and thoughts.

Your thoughts carry measurable energetic and neurological signatures. From a scientific perspective, thoughts influence your emotional state via neurotransmitters like dopamine and cortisol, which in turn affect your physical health, decision-making and behaviour [18]. Spiritual teachings often refer to this as "vibration", the frequency at which your inner world is resonating. In modern terms, it's your emotional-physiological signature.

Studies in affective neuroscience and somatic psychology show that chronic thought patterns, whether of gratitude, fear or self-doubt, create corresponding emotional states, which influence brain plasticity and behaviour over time [19]. This aligns with Dr Joe Dispenza's work on how repeated thoughts literally "wire" the brain and create consistent emotional-energetic states [20].

When you shift your thinking from fear to possibility, your "frequency" changes, not just spiritually but biologically. Gratitude, for example, has been shown to activate brain regions associated with emotional regulation and empathy, while reducing inflammation and increasing subjective well-being [21].

I experienced this principle vividly in my journey as a public speaker. When I first began speaking publicly, my thoughts were vibrating at a frequency of fear and self-consciousness. All I could think about was a humiliating Year 10 English presentation where my mouth went completely dry and my hands visibly trembled before the entire class. This memory created a powerful thought pattern that generated anxiety whenever I faced an audience.

Each time I approached the stage, my internal dialogue was filled with concerns about myself: "My voice will shake." "I'll forget what to say." "They'll see how nervous I am." These thoughts weren't just passive worries; they were creating an energetic frequency that manifested as physical symptoms and diminished performance.

The transformation began when I consciously shifted the frequency of my thoughts from self-concern to service. Instead of focusing on my fears, I deliberately tuned my thinking to "add value, add value" and directed my attention to "the one person in the audience who truly needed to hear this message". This wasn't just positive thinking – it was literally changing the vibrational frequency of my thoughts from fear to contribution.

The results were remarkable. As my thought frequency shifted, so did my physical experience and impact as a speaker. With each event, regardless of audience size or composition, I found myself needing to remind myself less often to "add value" or "find the one person". The higher-frequency thoughts became my natural pattern, creating a completely different speaking experience and audience connection.

Whether you view this through a spiritual lens or a neurological one, the principle remains the same: your thoughts change your biology, your behaviour and the reality you experience. Some call it the law of vibration; others refer to neuroplasticity or quantum resonance. Whatever the terminology, the takeaway is this: your inner frequency shapes your outer experience. The energy you emit, whether it's based on elevated emotions or fear-based states, sets the tone for what you resonate with and what resonates with you.

Chapter 4: The Power of Thoughts and Beliefs

This explains why, when you're having a "bad day", negative experiences seem to multiply. You've tuned in to what we might call "Negativity FM" and can only receive broadcasts on that frequency. The good news is that you can consciously change the station at any moment by deliberately choosing different thoughts.

By understanding the vibrational nature of thought, you gain a powerful tool for personal transformation. You're no longer at the mercy of random thinking but can consciously select thoughts that vibrate at the frequency of the reality you wish to create.

The Mind-Reality Connection

The connection between your mind and your external reality is perhaps the most transformative discovery on the journey of personal growth. Your thoughts are not merely passive observers of reality; they are active creators of it. Neuroscience reveals that what we perceive as reality is actually a construction of the brain, heavily influenced by our expectations and beliefs rather than a direct representation of the external world [22]. This mind-reality connection works in several ways:

1. **Perceptual Filtering**: Your thoughts determine what you notice and what you ignore. If you believe opportunities are scarce, you'll overlook abundant possibilities all around you.
2. **Interpretative Framework**: Your thoughts provide the framework through which you interpret events. The same situation can be seen as a disaster or an opportunity depending on your thought patterns.
3. **Behavioural Influence**: Your thoughts direct your actions, which produce tangible results in your physical

reality. Thoughts of capability lead to bold actions and thoughts of inadequacy lead to hesitation or inaction.
4. **Energetic Resonance**: As discussed earlier, your thoughts emit vibrations that attract matching experiences through the principle of resonance.

Consider this example: Two colleagues, Luna and Paul, are both passed over for a promotion they had hoped to receive. Luna, whose thought patterns tend towards limitation and personal inadequacy, immediately interprets this as confirmation that she's "not good enough" and "will never advance in her career". Her thoughts spiral into rumination about past failures, and she begins to disengage from her work. She stops volunteering for high-visibility projects and withdraws from team activities, convinced there's "no point in trying". Within six months, her performance review reflects her disengagement, further confirming her belief that she's inadequate.

Paul, however, whose thought patterns are oriented towards growth and possibility, has a markedly different experience. While initially disappointed, he thinks, "This is valuable feedback about areas where I can develop". He schedules a meeting with his manager to understand specifically which skills he needs to strengthen. He creates a development plan, seeks out a mentor and takes on challenging projects that build these capabilities. Within the same six months, he's positioned himself as a stronger candidate for the next opportunity and feels more engaged and valued in his current role.

Same external circumstance (being passed over for promotion), yet entirely different outcomes based solely on their thought patterns and the resulting actions. This example isn't about toxic

Chapter 4: The Power of Thoughts and Beliefs

positivity or denying disappointment; it's about recognising the power of your interpretive framework to shape your subsequent reality.

The Mental Faculties that Shape Perception

To harness the power of your thoughts effectively, it's essential to understand the mental faculties that govern them. These faculties are like muscles; they strengthen with use and atrophy with neglect. The primary mental faculties include:

1. **Perception**: Your ability to become aware of your environment through your physical senses and intuition.
2. **Reason**: Your ability to think logically, make connections and draw conclusions based on evidence.
3. **Will**: Your ability to focus attention and direct mental energy towards specific thoughts and goals.
4. **Memory**: Your ability to store and recall information and experiences.
5. **Imagination**: Your ability to form mental images of things not present to your senses or not yet existing.
6. **Intuition**: Your ability to understand something immediately, without conscious reasoning.

Of these, imagination deserves special attention. Einstein famously said, "Imagination is more important than knowledge," recognising that while knowledge is limited to what is already known, imagination embraces the entire world and all there ever will be to know and understand.

Your imagination is the creative faculty of the mind, the aspect that allows you to envision possibilities beyond your current reality. By consciously directing your imagination towards what you wish to create rather than what you fear, you harness one of the most powerful faculties for transforming your thought patterns and, consequently, your beliefs and reality.

The "You Are the Sky; Your Thoughts Are the Weather" Metaphor

One of the most illuminating metaphors for understanding the relationship between you and your thoughts comes from Buddhist philosophy: "You are the sky; your thoughts are the weather." This perspective of creating distance between oneself and one's thoughts is central to mindfulness-based approaches that have shown remarkable effectiveness in reducing suffering.

This metaphor beautifully captures several essential truths:

1. **Thoughts Are Temporary**: Like weather patterns, thoughts come and go. Even the most intense storm eventually passes, just as the most intense thought or emotion will naturally subside if not fed with continued attention.
2. **You Are the Observer**: You are not your thoughts; you are the awareness that observes them. Just as the sky remains unchanged regardless of whether it's experiencing sunshine, rain or storms, your essential nature remains whole and undiminished regardless of the thoughts passing through your mind.
3. **Expansiveness vs. Contraction**: The sky represents your natural state of expansive awareness, while turbulent weather represents the contraction that occurs when you identify with limiting thoughts.

Chapter 4: The Power of Thoughts and Beliefs

4. **Perspective Matters**: From the ground, we may see only storm clouds and miss the clear blue sky beyond. Similarly, when caught in negative thought patterns, we may forget our capacity for clarity and peace.

This metaphor provides not just understanding but a practical approach to working with thoughts. When troubling thoughts arise, you can mentally step back and observe them as passing weather while remaining anchored in the vast sky of your awareness. This practice alone can transform your relationship with your thoughts, reducing their control over your emotional state and actions.

Practical Exercises for Thought Transformation

Understanding the power of thoughts and beliefs is merely the first step. To create lasting change, you must put this understanding into practice through consistent mental exercises. Here are several powerful practices for transforming your thought patterns:

1. **Thought Awareness**: For one week, carry a small notebook or use a notes app on your phone. Each time you notice a negative or limiting thought, write it down. This practice alone often reduces the thought's power by bringing it from the subconscious into conscious awareness.
2. **Thought Questioning**: Using the Byron Katie method, ask four questions about each limiting belief:
    - Is it true?
    - Can I absolutely know it's true?
    - How do I react when I believe this thought?
    - Who would I be without this thought?

3. **Thought Replacement**: Identify your most common negative thoughts and create positive alternatives. For example, replace "I'm not good enough" with "I am constantly growing and improving".
4. **Visualisation**: Spend 10 minutes each morning visualising yourself embodying your desired beliefs and living your ideal reality. Engage all your senses to make the visualisation as vivid as possible.
5. **Affirmations with Feeling**: Create affirmations that resonate emotionally and repeat them with genuine feeling. Remember, it's the emotional charge that accelerates belief formation.
6. **Gratitude Practice**: Each evening, write down three things you're grateful for. This simple practice shifts your thought patterns towards appreciation and abundance.
7. **Mindful Observation**: Practise observing your thoughts without judgement or attachment. This creates space between you and your thoughts, reducing their automatic influence.
8. **The Thought Control Exercise**: This is a powerful demonstration of your ability to direct your thoughts at will.

Try this exercise I use regularly in my workshops:

Close your eyes. Think of a can of Coke. Picture it clearly in your mind: its red colour, the condensation on the outside, perhaps the fizzing sound as you open it.

Now, change that image. If you imagined a red can, make it silver (Diet Coke). If you visualised a silver can, make it red. You've just taken control over your thoughts.

Chapter 4: The Power of Thoughts and Beliefs

Next, completely remove the can of Coke from your mind and instead visualise a unicorn. See its mane, its horn, the colours – make it as detailed as possible.

Then change the colour of the unicorn and its mane.

Now, make that unicorn ride a rainbow. Add more details, colours, movement.

Finally, shift your thoughts to the happiest memory of your life. It could be a person, a place, an achievement – whatever brings you joy. Make this image as big, bright and colourful as possible. Notice what you see, hear, smell, taste and feel in this memory. Let the positive emotions expand throughout your body.

Open your eyes.

Congratulations!

You've just taken complete control over your thoughts.

Most people walking this planet have no idea they can do this. You've shown that you can create thoughts out of nothing (when was the last time you randomly thought about unicorns?), change existing thoughts and direct your mental energy towards positive emotional states.

This is the foundation of thought mastery.

The key to success with these exercises is consistency. Just as physical muscles develop through regular exercise, your mental faculties strengthen through daily practice.

Commitment to these exercises, even when results aren't immediately visible, is essential for creating lasting transformation.

The Ripple Effect of Transformed Thoughts

When you change your thoughts, you change far more than just your mental activity. The effects ripple through every aspect of the Identity Wheel and, ultimately, your life experience:

Identity → Thoughts → Beliefs → Emotions → Actions → Results → Identity Confirmation

As your thoughts transform, your emotions naturally follow. You cannot hold thoughts of abundance and feel scarcity simultaneously. You cannot entertain thoughts of self-worth and feel inadequate at the same time. Your emotional landscape is a direct reflection of your thought patterns.

Your transformed thoughts and emotions lead to different actions. When you think and feel differently, you naturally behave differently, often without conscious effort. Someone who believes "I am capable" approaches challenges with confidence and perseverance, while someone who believes "I am inadequate" approaches the same challenges with hesitation and premature surrender.

These different actions produce different results, which then circle back to confirm or challenge your core identity. This is how thought transformation initiates a positive spiral that eventually rewrites your entire life narrative.

Chapter 4: The Power of Thoughts and Beliefs

The Promise of Thought Mastery

As we conclude this exploration of the power of thoughts and beliefs, we arrive at a fundamental truth: mastering your thoughts is the master key to personal transformation. When you gain conscious control over your thought patterns, you essentially take the wheel of your life's direction.

This mastery doesn't mean you'll never experience negative thoughts again. Rather, it means you no longer remain at their mercy. You develop the capacity to observe thoughts without automatically believing or acting on them. You cultivate the discernment to distinguish between thoughts that serve your growth and those that hinder it.

The journey towards thought mastery is lifelong, with ever-deepening layers of awareness and intention. Each step frees you from limiting patterns and opens new access to your creative potential. The Identity Wheel keeps turning, but with conscious thought mastery *you* take the wheel.

When you understand your power to direct your thoughts, you stop being a passenger in your own mind. You become the artist of your reality. And as we'll see next, your emotional world – the very fuel of your actions – is the canvas where those thoughts come to life.

For now, remember this: your thoughts are the seeds of your future reality. Choose them wisely, nurture them consciously and watch as they grow into the life you truly desire.

Looking Ahead

Now that we understand the power of thoughts and beliefs in shaping our reality, we're ready to explore how these elements create our emotional experience. In the next chapter, we'll discover how to master your emotional landscape and recognise emotions as valuable feedback rather than dictators of your actions, learning to regulate your emotional state and harnessing emotional energy to fuel positive transformation.

Chapter 4: The Power of Thoughts and Beliefs

Chapter Summary

Thoughts bridge identity to emotions with recurring thoughts crystallising into beliefs.

Beliefs are thoughts you've kept thinking without challenge, often without factual proof.

Thoughts have a vibrational nature, resonating at different frequencies that affect your body, emotions and reality.

Thoughts evolve into beliefs through exposure, repetition, emotional attachment, evidence gathering, belief crystallisation and identity integration.

Limiting beliefs can be transformed through gathering evidence, questioning origins, testing reality, finding counterexamples and creating new beliefs.

The Law of Vibration explains how thoughts change your biology, behaviour and reality.

Mind-reality connection works through perceptual filtering, interpretative framework, behavioural influence and energetic resonance.

Practical thought exercises like thought awareness, questioning, replacement, visualisation and gratitude create lasting transformation.

The Identity Wheel

REFLECTION QUESTIONS

1. What recurring thought patterns do you notice throughout your day? Which ones serve you, and which ones limit you?
2. How have your thoughts about a situation changed the experience itself? Can you recall a time when shifting your perspective completely transformed an experience?
3. Which mental faculty (perception, reason, will, memory, imagination, intuition) do you rely on most heavily? Which might you benefit from strengthening?

PRACTICAL EXERCISES

1. Thought Tracking

- For one day, carry a small notebook or use your phone
- Each time you notice a negative or limiting thought, write it down
- At the end of the day, look for patterns:
    - Are certain situations triggering specific thought patterns?
    - Are there recurring themes or concerns?
    - How do these thoughts influence your emotions and actions?

2. Thought Questioning

- Select one recurring limiting thought
- Ask yourself:
    - Is this thought absolutely true? (Can I be 100% certain?)

Chapter 4: The Power of Thoughts and Beliefs

- What evidence suggests this thought might not be completely accurate?
- What perspective am I missing?
- How would I view this situation if it were happening to someone I care about?

3. Mental Faculty Development

- Choose one mental faculty you'd like to strengthen:
    - Perception: Practise observing details in your environment
    - Reason: Analyse a situation from multiple logical perspectives
    - Will: Focus on completing one task without distraction
    - Memory: Practise recalling details from a recent experience
    - Imagination: Visualise a desired outcome in vivid detail
    - Intuition: Listen to your gut feeling about a decision
- Spend 5-10 minutes daily for one week exercising this faculty

Chapter 5: Mastering Your Emotional Landscape

In the previous chapters, we've explored how the Identity Wheel shows the cyclical nature of our identity, thoughts, emotions, actions and results. We've examined the architecture of the mind that powers this wheel, and we've delved into the power of our thoughts and beliefs in shaping our reality. Now, we turn our attention to what is perhaps the most immediate and instinctive element of our experience: our emotional landscape.

Emotions are often misunderstood as unpredictable forces that happen to us like random weather patterns we must simply endure. But as we'll discover in this chapter, our emotional state is neither random nor beyond our influence. Just as a skilled meteorologist can read the signs in the atmosphere to predict tomorrow's weather, you can learn to understand the patterns of your emotional world and, more importantly, influence its climate.

You can't control your first emotional response to a situation, but you can control your second. The first response is automatic; the second response is a choice. Your character is built in the space between the two.

The Emotional Barometer of Thought Patterns

Picture yourself waking up on a Monday morning. As you wake up, your mind begins its familiar monologue: "Another week begins. So much to do. I'm already exhausted just thinking about it." Almost instantly, you feel a heaviness in your chest, a tightness in your shoulders and a general sense of dread washes over you.

What happened here? The thoughts about the week ahead directly triggered an emotional response. This is the emotional barometer at work, providing instant feedback about your thought patterns. Like a finely calibrated instrument, your emotions are constantly reflecting the quality and nature of your thinking.

This intimate relationship between thoughts and emotions is the foundation of emotional mastery. Your thoughts will always lead to your feelings, but as we discussed in previous chapters, these thoughts often operate at a subconscious level (they're part of your programming), running silently in the background of your mind. These are past thoughts you're holding onto that are causing your current feelings and emotions, even when you're not actively aware of them.

Let's explore this further through a simple example. Tess and Michael both receive the same constructive feedback from their manager on a project. Tess immediately thinks, "I knew I'd mess this up. I'm just not good at this job." This thought pattern triggers feelings of shame, inadequacy and anxiety. Michael, however, thinks, "Interesting feedback. This gives me a clear direction for

Chapter 5: Mastering Your Emotional Landscape

improvement." His thought pattern generates feelings of curiosity, determination and even slight excitement about the opportunity to grow.

Same external circumstance, vastly different emotional responses, all determined by their respective thought patterns.

The crucial insight here is that your emotional response is not directly caused by external events but by your interpretation of those events. This interpretation happens through your thoughts, which are heavily influenced by your identity (those core "I am" statements we explored in Chapter 3).

Dr Joe Dispenza's groundbreaking research offers fascinating insights into this mechanism. According to Dr Dispenza, we can literally train our bodies to feel certain emotions through repetitive thinking. When we repeatedly think certain thoughts, our bodies produce corresponding biochemical reactions by releasing specific neurotransmitters and hormones that create particular feeling states. Over time, these biochemical states become familiar to the body, and we develop what Dr Dispenza calls an "emotional addiction" to these states.

Through his work with brain imaging and measuring neurochemical changes, Dr Dispenza has shown that the body doesn't distinguish between an emotion created by an actual experience and one created by thought alone. This explains why merely thinking about a stressful situation can trigger the same physiological stress response as actually experiencing it.

This is where science and spirituality meet. Ancient traditions have long taught that we can influence our emotional state through thought, meditation and intention, and now neuroscience is beginning to confirm it. Whether you describe it as mental rehearsal, energetic alignment or rewiring your brain, the result is the same: your inner world shapes your emotional chemistry [23].

And when you shift your emotional baseline, every spoke of the Identity Wheel starts to turn in a new direction.

Your emotional barometer doesn't merely react to conscious thoughts. It's constantly taking readings from the totality of your mental activity, including those deeply embedded subconscious patterns. This is why you might sometimes feel anxious, sad or angry without any obvious trigger. Your emotional barometer is simply reflecting thought patterns running beneath the surface of conscious awareness.

Emotions as Feedback, Not Facts

One of the most transformative shifts in understanding emotions is recognising them as valuable feedback rather than irrefutable facts about reality. Emotions are data, not directives [24].

Your emotions aren't trying to control you; they're trying to inform you.

When your car's dashboard displays a warning light, you don't curse the light or try to cover it with tape (or maybe you do?). You recognise it as valuable information about the state of your vehicle and take appropriate action. Similarly, emotions are your mind's way of communicating important information about your internal state.

Chapter 5: Mastering Your Emotional Landscape

Consider anxiety. Many people experience anxiety as an overwhelming negative state that must be escaped or suppressed. But what if we viewed anxiety as simply information? What might that anxiety be telling you? Perhaps it's signalling that:

- You're operating outside your comfort zone (which might be exactly where growth happens)
- You care deeply about the outcome of a situation
- You need more preparation or information
- A boundary is being crossed
- Your values are being compromised

By reframing emotions as feedback rather than facts or commands, we create space to respond thoughtfully rather than react automatically. This doesn't mean that emotions aren't sometimes intensely uncomfortable; they absolutely can be. But understanding them as information rather than emergencies changes our relationship with them.

A student I worked with at a PRU school (Pupil Referral Unit – provides education for children who are unable to attend mainstream schools) who struggled with intense anger issues discovered this distinction during our sessions together. Whenever he felt angry, he would immediately act on that anger, believing it was commanding him to express it, often in destructive ways. Through our work, he learned to view his anger as information. "My anger is telling me something important," he began to say, "but it's not telling me what to do about it".

This shift allowed him to ask questions like: "What is this anger informing me about? Is a boundary being crossed? Am I feeling powerless or disrespected? What unmet need is behind this anger?" These questions transformed his relationship with anger from one of helpless reactivity to thoughtful response.

The Emotions Wheel: Identifying Specific Emotions

To master your emotional landscape, you need more refined language than simply "good" or "bad", "positive" or "negative." Most of us use broad, generic terms to describe our emotional states, which limits our ability to understand and work with them effectively.

The Emotions Wheel, developed by psychologist Dr Robert Plutchik, offers a more nuanced vocabulary for our emotional experiences. At its centre are eight primary emotions: joy, trust, fear, surprise, sadness, disgust, anger and anticipation. These branch outward into more specific emotions, creating a rich map of human emotional experience. When we can accurately name our emotions, we gain greater insight into their causes and appropriate responses. There's a vast difference between feeling disappointed and feeling devastated, between feeling irritated and feeling enraged, or between feeling content and feeling elated. Yet we often lump these distinct experiences into vague categories like "bad" or "good".

Chapter 5: Mastering Your Emotional Landscape

Using the Emotions Wheel in Practice

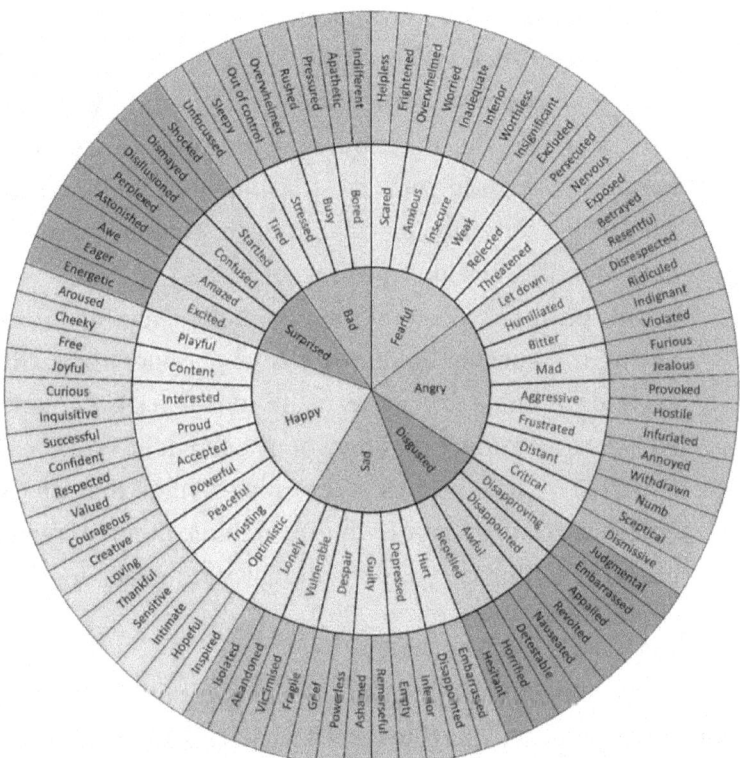

Here's how to effectively use the Emotions Wheel in your daily life:

1. **Start at the centre**: When you notice a strong emotion, begin with the core emotions in the centre of the wheel. Ask yourself: "Is this closer to anger, fear, sadness, disgust, surprise, anticipation, joy or trust?"
2. **Move outward**: Once you've identified the general category, move to the middle ring for more specificity. For example, if you've identified "anger" as your core emotion, is it more like humiliation, let down or distant?

The Identity Wheel

3. **Reach the outer ring**: Continue to the outermost ring for the most precise identification. That "humiliation" might actually be more specifically described as feeling disrespected, betrayed or withdrawn.
4. **Notice physical sensations**: Pay attention to where and how you feel the emotion in your body. Anger might manifest as heat in your chest, while anxiety might create a fluttering sensation in your stomach. These physical cues help identify emotions more accurately.
5. **Track patterns**: Keep a simple emotion log for a week, noting the specific emotions you experience throughout each day. Look for patterns in what triggers certain emotions and how they affect your behaviour.
6. **Practise with others**: Try identifying the specific emotions of characters while watching films or reading books. This builds your emotional vocabulary in a low-stakes environment.

Consider how this more refined emotional vocabulary might help in a practical situation. Imagine you're preparing for an important presentation and feeling "Anxious". That's a start, but it's quite vague. Using the Emotions Wheel, you might discover that what you're actually feeling is:

Nervous (afraid of judgement)

Inadequate (concerned about your competence)

Excited (anticipating positive outcomes)

Overwhelmed (feeling the weight of expectations)

Chapter 5: Mastering Your Emotional Landscape

Each of these more specific emotions points to different underlying thoughts and beliefs, and each might call for a different response. Feeling vulnerable might be addressed through self-compassion practices, while feeling unprepared might be resolved through additional preparation or practice.

The more precisely you can identify your emotions, the more effectively you can address their underlying causes and choose appropriate responses.

However many people still struggle to name what they're feeling, even with the emotions wheel.

When Words Aren't Enough: Feeling Through Colour and Shape

Sometimes, words aren't enough to capture how we really feel.

Language tries to put boundaries around something that's often fluid, messy and alive. And for many people, especially those who are neurodivergent, dealing with trauma or just not used to emotional vocabulary, finding the right word can feel impossible.

When I first started working with SEND (Special Educational Needs and Disabilities) students, I realised how much they struggled to articulate their emotions using traditional tools like the emotions wheel. So I adapted.

Instead of asking, *"How are you feeling?"* I asked, *"If your feeling was a colour, what colour would it be?"* *"If it had a shape, what shape would it have?"*

It sounds simple, and it is. But it works.

The Identity Wheel

Because sometimes, a feeling isn't just "sad" or "anxious". Sometimes it feels like a deep, heavy blue. Or like a sharp, spiky triangle. Or like a heavy cloud sitting on your chest.

This approach isn't just for SEND students. It works just as powerfully with neurotypical adults. It taps into a part of us that's pre-verbal, a part that's honest without needing to explain itself.

Personally, when I notice my mental health starting to dip, I don't always have the perfect word for it. But I feel it: *prickly*. It's a sensation that means something very specific to me. It's a warning sign.
It tells me it's time to pause, to check in, to pull out the tools from my mental health toolbox before things spiral further.

Your version might be different. Maybe you feel a dense fog, or a tangled knot, or a burning fire. The specifics don't matter; what matters is that **you** understand it. That you honour it. That you learn to listen to your inner signals, even when words fail.

Emotions speak many languages. Colour, shape, texture: These are just different ways your subconscious communicates with you.

Learning to hear those signals, in whatever form they come, is one of the most powerful steps you can take towards self-awareness, resilience and healing.

Emotional Weather Patterns as a Visualisation Tool

Just as the Earth has weather patterns, your emotional life has recognisable patterns that play out over time. These patterns aren't random but are the result of habitual thought patterns combined with life circumstances and physical states.

Chapter 5: Mastering Your Emotional Landscape

Visualising your emotions as weather patterns can be a powerful tool for understanding their temporary nature and your relationship to them. Consider these parallels:

Emotional Storms: Intense but temporary periods of strong emotion, often triggered by significant events or stress. Like a thunderstorm, these pass, even though they may feel overwhelming in the moment.

Emotional Climate: Your general emotional tendency over time. Are you generally sunny and optimistic or prone to cloudy periods of melancholy? This climate is largely shaped by your identity and habitual thought patterns.

Emotional Seasons: Longer periods of particular emotional tendencies, often connected to life circumstances or developmental stages. Just as winter eventually yields to spring, difficult emotional seasons do pass.

The weather metaphor also reminds us that we are not our emotions, just as the sky is not the weather passing through it. You are the vast, unchanging awareness through which emotional states pass. This perspective creates a liberating distance between you and your emotions.

This doesn't mean suppressing or denying emotions but rather changing your relationship with them. You can acknowledge the presence of an emotional storm while remembering that you are the vast sky through which it passes.

Identifying Unmet Needs Behind Emotions

Every emotion, particularly those we find difficult or uncomfortable, contains within it information about our needs, both met and unmet. Anger often signals violated boundaries or unmet needs for respect. Sadness frequently points to losses or unmet needs for connection. Fear typically indicates threats or unmet needs for safety and security.

Understanding the needs behind our emotions transforms them from seemingly irrational reactions into meaningful signals about what matters to us. This understanding can guide us towards constructive action rather than impulsive reaction.

Consider the following examples:

- When you feel irritated by a colleague's interruptions, the unmet need might be for focus or respect.
- When you feel disappointed about not being invited to a social gathering, the unmet need might be for inclusion or significance.
- When you feel anxious about an upcoming presentation, the unmet need might be for preparation or validation.

By identifying the needs behind your emotions, you gain clarity about what action might genuinely resolve the situation, rather than merely attempting to escape the uncomfortable feeling.

Emma, an A&E nurse, described a transformational moment using this approach: "I was feeling intensely frustrated with my team, and my default would have been to send a stern email demanding better performance. Instead, I asked myself what need was unmet

Chapter 5: Mastering Your Emotional Landscape

and realised I was feeling unheard and unappreciated. Rather than sending that email, I scheduled a team meeting where I could share my vision more clearly and create space for genuine collaboration. The result was so much more productive than my initial impulse."

The link between emotions and needs also helps explain why certain emotional patterns persist in our lives. If we don't address the underlying needs, we'll continue to experience the emotional signals. Attempting to suppress or ignore emotions without addressing the needs they highlight is like continually resetting a smoke alarm without investigating the fire.

Techniques for Emotional Regulation

Understanding the nature of emotions is essential, but equally important are practical techniques for regulating them, especially when they threaten to overwhelm us. Emotional regulation doesn't mean suppression or denial; it means developing the capacity to experience emotions without being controlled by them.

Here are several proven techniques for emotional regulation:

1. The 90-Second Rule: Neuroanatomist Dr Jill Bolte Taylor discovered that the physiological response of an emotion (the chemical cascade triggered by a thought) typically lasts about 90 seconds. After that, any continued emotional response is due to choosing to stay in that emotional loop through thought. This means that if you can observe an emotion for just 90 seconds without feeding it with additional thoughts, its intensity will naturally begin to diminish.[27]

2. Box Breathing: A powerful technique used by Navy SEALs and other high-performance individuals, box breathing directly impacts your nervous system, helping to calm the fight-or-flight response. Inhale for a count of four, hold for four, exhale for four, hold for four, and repeat. This simple practice can shift your physiological state in moments.

3. Emotional Distancing: This involves observing your emotions from a slightly detached perspective. Instead of saying "I am angry", try "I notice anger arising" or "There is anger present". This subtle linguistic shift creates space between you and the emotion, allowing for a more thoughtful response.

4. The RAIN Process: Developed by meditation teacher Tara Brach, RAIN stands for:

- **Recognise** what is happening
- **Allow** the experience to be there, just as it is
- **Investigate** with interest and care
- **Nurture** with self-compassion

This process guides you through acknowledging emotions, accepting their presence without judgement, exploring them with curiosity and responding to yourself with kindness.[28]

5. Physical Movement: Emotions generate energy in the body, and movement helps process and release this energy. Even a brief walk, stretch or change in posture can shift your emotional state by changing your physiology [29].

These techniques aren't about controlling emotions in the sense of forcing them to change. Rather, they're about creating conditions

Chapter 5: Mastering Your Emotional Landscape

that allow emotions to move through you naturally without getting stuck or escalating unnecessarily.

Creating an Empowering Emotional State

While emotions often arise spontaneously, we're not entirely at their mercy. Through deliberate practices, we can cultivate emotional states that support our goals and well-being. This means intentionally nurturing emotional states that serve you whilst honouring authentic feelings

Here are strategies for creating empowering emotional states:

1. Gratitude Practice: Research consistently shows that regularly focusing on what you appreciate creates measurable shifts in emotional well-being. By directing attention towards what's good in your life, you literally tune your brain to notice more positive aspects of your experience.

2. Visualisation: Elite athletes use visualisation not just to rehearse physical movements but also to generate specific emotional states associated with peak performance. By vividly imagining scenarios where you feel confident, peaceful or joyful, you create neural patterns that make these states more accessible.

3. Embodiment Practices: Your physiology and emotions are intricately connected. By changing your posture, breathing, facial expressions and movement patterns, you can directly influence your emotional state. Amy Cuddy's research on "power posing" shows how even brief physical adjustments can create measurable hormonal changes associated with confidence and reduced stress [30]. We will cover this in more detail in the next chapter.

4. Environment Design: Your physical environment significantly impacts your emotional state. Intentionally designing spaces that evoke your desired emotional states (through colour, light, organisation, nature elements, meaningful objects or music) creates a container that supports emotional well-being.

5. Relationship Cultivation: The people you spend time with profoundly influence your emotional patterns. Cultivating relationships with people who embody the emotional qualities you wish to develop naturally shifts your own emotional tendencies through the principle of resonance.

These practices aren't about achieving some idealised emotional state where you never experience difficult feelings. Rather, they're about expanding your emotional range and resilience, making empowering states more accessible while developing greater capacity to work with challenging emotions when they arise.

Jess, a former client who struggled with chronic anxiety, transformed her emotional landscape through consistent practice of these techniques. "I used to wake up anxious every morning," she explained. "Now I start each day with gratitude and visualisation. I've redesigned my home office with colours and images that make me feel calm and inspired. I'm still the same person, I still feel anxiety sometimes, but it's no longer the dominant note in my emotional symphony."

The Connection Between Emotions and Action

As we explore the Identity Wheel, we see how emotions form the crucial bridge between thoughts and actions. While thoughts

Chapter 5: Mastering Your Emotional Landscape

influence our emotions, it's our emotions that often drive our behaviours, either propelling us forward or holding us back.

When we feel confident and inspired, taking bold action comes naturally. When we feel fearful or discouraged, even simple actions can seem insurmountable. This is why emotional mastery is not merely about feeling better, it's about creating an emotional foundation that supports effective action.

Consider two people with the same goal of starting a business. Both have similar skills, resources and opportunities. However, one consistently feels excited, confident and determined, while the other frequently experiences doubt, worry and overwhelm. Which person is more likely to take the necessary actions to succeed?

The relationship between emotions and action works in both directions. Emotions influence actions, but actions also influence emotions. This creates the opportunity for a powerful intervention: when you can't directly change how you feel, you can often change how you act, which in turn shifts your emotional state.

Katie, a talented writer who struggled with procrastination, discovered this bidirectional relationship during our work together. "I was waiting to feel motivated before I would write," she explained. "I thought the feeling had to come first. Then I experimented with writing for just 15 minutes regardless of how I felt. Remarkably, the act of writing often generated the motivation I was waiting for. Action first, emotion second, it was a complete paradigm shift."

This insight creates a pathway out of emotional states that might otherwise trap us in inaction. You don't need to feel confident to act confidently. You don't need to feel motivated to take motivated action. By acting "as if" you already embody your desired emotional state, you often begin to generate that very state.

Emotional Patterns and the Identity Wheel

Let's return to the Identity Wheel to understand how emotional mastery fits into the larger pattern of personal transformation. As we've explored throughout this book, the wheel illustrates how our identity creates thoughts, thoughts generate emotions, emotions drive actions and actions produce results, which then either confirm or challenge our identity.

Emotions are the crucial link in this chain, determining whether our thoughts will translate into effective action or remain mere wishful thinking. When we master our emotional landscape, we ensure that our thoughts and beliefs can manifest as the actions and results we desire.

Consider this example: Curtis identifies as "not a natural public speaker" (identity). When asked to present at a conference, he thinks, "I'll probably make a fool of myself" (thoughts). These thoughts generate feelings of anxiety and inadequacy (emotions). These uncomfortable emotions lead him to minimally prepare and rush through his presentation (actions). His poor performance generates negative feedback (results), which confirms his original identity: "See? I'm not a natural public speaker."

Through emotional mastery, Curtis could interrupt this cycle. While his identity and initial thoughts might be the same, he could

Chapter 5: Mastering Your Emotional Landscape

work with the resulting anxiety differently. Rather than being overwhelmed by it, he might recognise it as natural nervous energy that can be channelled into thorough preparation. By regulating his emotional response, he creates the possibility of different actions (careful preparation, practice, seeking feedback) and consequently different results, which might begin to challenge his limiting identity.

This is the power of emotional mastery within the Identity Wheel; it creates a pivot point where the entire cycle can begin to shift in a more empowering direction.

The Promise of Emotional Mastery

As we conclude this exploration of the emotional landscape, let's reflect on what becomes possible when you master this crucial domain of human experience.

Emotional mastery doesn't mean never experiencing difficult emotions as that would be neither possible nor desirable. The rich tapestry of human emotions, including the challenging ones, gives life its depth and meaning. Rather, emotional mastery means developing a wise and skilful relationship with your full emotional spectrum.

When you master your emotional landscape, you gain:

- **Freedom from emotional reactivity**: You respond thoughtfully rather than react automatically to triggering situations.
- **Emotional resilience**: You recover more quickly from setbacks and difficulties.

- **Access to intuitive wisdom**: You can distinguish between emotions as reactions versus emotions as intuitive guidance.
- **Authentic connection**: You relate to others from emotional authenticity rather than habitual patterns.
- **Expanded capacity**: You develop the ability to hold more intense emotions without becoming overwhelmed.
- **Creative power**: You channel emotional energy into creative expression and purposeful action.

These capacities don't develop overnight but emerge gradually through consistent practice and self-compassion. Each time you apply the principles and techniques we've explored, you strengthen your emotional muscles, just as physical exercise strengthens your body.

Remember that the goal isn't to reach some idealised state of perpetual happiness or calm. Such a state doesn't exist and wouldn't serve you if it did. The goal is to develop a fluid, responsive relationship with your emotions to be able to fully experience their messages and energy while not being controlled by them.

As you continue this journey, approach your emotional landscape with curiosity rather than judgement. Each emotion, even the most challenging, carries wisdom when approached with awareness. The very emotions you might have once avoided may become your greatest teachers and allies in creating the life you truly desire.

Chapter 5: Mastering Your Emotional Landscape

Looking Ahead

Emotional mastery isn't about avoiding difficult feelings; it's about learning to respond to them with awareness, wisdom and intention. As you've seen, your emotions are powerful feedback systems, not enemies to be suppressed. They are the fuel that drives your actions or stalls them.

But there's one emotion that quietly underpins most inaction, hesitation and self-sabotage: fear. It's the silent saboteur that often disguises itself as logic, caution or "just being realistic".

In the next chapter, we'll explore fear not as something to conquer but as something to understand, deeply and compassionately. You'll discover how fear interacts with your beliefs, your identity and your habits, and how, when embraced correctly, it becomes a gateway to courage and forward movement.

Get ready to transform your relationship with fear. Because when fear no longer drives your decisions, aligned action becomes inevitable.

Chapter Summary

Emotions serve as a barometer providing instant feedback about your thought patterns.

Emotions are feedback, not facts – valuable information rather than irrefutable truths about reality.

The Emotions Wheel provides nuanced vocabulary for identifying specific emotions beyond "good" or "bad".

Emotional weather patterns help visualise the temporary nature of emotions and your relationship to them.

Unmet needs lie behind difficult emotions, providing crucial information about what matters to you.

Emotional regulation techniques include the 90-Second Rule, Box Breathing, Emotional Distancing, the RAIN Process and Physical Movement.

Empowering emotional states can be cultivated through gratitude, visualisation, embodiment practices, environment design and relationship cultivation.

Emotions bridge thoughts to actions, determining whether knowledge will translate into effective behaviour.

Chapter 5: Mastering Your Emotional Landscape

REFLECTION QUESTIONS

1. How would you describe your relationship with your emotions? Do you tend to suppress them, get overwhelmed by them, or use them as information?
2. Which emotions do you find most challenging to experience? What beliefs might be behind this resistance?
3. How might your life change if you viewed emotions as valuable messengers rather than states to be controlled?

PRACTICAL EXERCISES

1. Emotional Vocabulary Expansion

- Create your personal emotions wheel:
    - Draw three concentric circles
    - In the inner circle, write the basic emotions (joy, fear, anger, sadness, disgust, surprise)
    - In the middle circle, write more specific variations of each
    - In the outer circle, write the most precise emotional states
- Next time you feel something strongly, use this wheel to identify the specific emotion

2. Emotion-Thought Connection

- For the next three emotional experiences:
    - Name the emotion as specifically as possible
    - Identify the thought that preceded this feeling
    - Note the physical sensations associated with this emotion

- Ask: "What information is this emotion providing?"
  - Consider: "What need might be behind this emotion?"

3. Emotional Weather Observation

- Create a simple emotional weather journal for one week
- Each day, note:
  - Your predominant emotional "weather" (sunny, cloudy, stormy, etc.)
  - Any significant emotional "events" (thunderstorms, rainbows, fog, etc.)
  - How you responded to these conditions
- At the end of the week, look for patterns in your emotional climate

Chapter 6: Beyond Fear – Reclaiming Your Power

In the previous chapters, we've explored how the Identity Wheel shows the cyclical nature of our identity, thoughts, emotions, actions and results. We've examined the architecture of the mind that powers this wheel, delved into our core identity statements, explored the power of our thoughts and beliefs, and learned how to master our emotional landscape. Now, we turn our attention to what is perhaps the most powerful force that keeps us trapped in limiting cycles: fear.

Fear is the invisible barrier that stands between who we are and who we're capable of becoming. It's the shadow that falls across our path just as we're about to step into our potential. Understanding and transforming your relationship with fear isn't just another step on the journey; it's the gateway to reclaiming your power and creating lasting change in your life.

The Nature of Fear: Understanding the Guardian at the Gate

Fear is a complex emotional state that serves as both protector and prison guard in our lives. At its most fundamental level, fear is a biological response designed to keep us safe from harm. This primal fear (the instinct that once saved our ancestors from predators and physical dangers) still resides within our brain's limbic system, specifically the amygdala [31].

However, in our modern world, this ancient survival mechanism has evolved beyond physical threats to include psychological, social and existential fears: fear of failure, fear of rejection, fear of the unknown, fear of success, fear of not being enough and, perhaps the most insidious, the fear of our own power [32].

There's a profound scene in the film Coach Carter where Samuel L. Jackson's character repeatedly asks one of his players, Timo Cruz, "What is your deepest fear?" Eventually, Cruz stands up and delivers a powerful response, quoting Marianne Williamson:

"Our deepest fear is not that we are inadequate. Our deepest fear is that we are powerful beyond measure. It is our light, not our darkness, that most frightens us."

This insight cuts to the heart of our most fundamental resistance to change. We don't just fear failing or being rejected, we fear what might happen if we actually succeed, if we step fully into our power, if we become the person we're truly capable of becoming. This fear of our own greatness can be more paralysing than any fear of inadequacy, because it challenges our entire sense of self and forces us to take responsibility for our vast potential [33].

Chapter 6: Beyond Fear – Reclaiming Your Power

The thing you're most afraid to lose is often the very thing that's preventing you from getting what you actually want.

Think about the last time you felt fear holding you back. Perhaps you wanted to express a brilliant idea in a meeting but remained silent, fearing judgement. Maybe you dreamed of starting a business but couldn't take the first step, paralysed by the fear of failure. Or perhaps you've felt drawn to transform your identity in some meaningful way, only to retreat back to the familiar when the discomfort of change becomes too intense.

In each of these instances, fear isn't protecting you from actual danger, it's protecting you from growth. The very mechanism designed to ensure your survival is now limiting your ability to thrive.

What makes fear particularly challenging is that it doesn't announce itself as fear. Instead, it disguises itself as rational thought, as protection, as wisdom. "I'm just being realistic," we tell ourselves. "I'm being prudent," we rationalise. But often these are simply sophisticated masks that fear wears to keep us safely within the boundaries of our comfort zone.

Fear and the Identity Wheel: Breaking the Cycle

To understand how fear fits into the Identity Wheel framework, let's examine how it influences each element of the cycle:

Identity → Fear: When we hold limiting identity statements ("I am not good enough", "I am not creative", "I am not worthy of success") these generate fear whenever we face opportunities that challenge these beliefs. Our identity creates a gravitational field that fear orbits around.

Thoughts → Fear: Our thoughts about the future, particularly catastrophic predictions and "what if" scenarios, trigger fear responses that feel as real as if the imagined dangers were actually happening. The brain doesn't distinguish between vividly imagined threats and real ones.

Fear → Emotions: Fear rarely travels alone. It brings with it a constellation of related emotional states: anxiety, worry, doubt, hesitation and even seemingly unrelated emotions like anger or apathy, which often mask underlying fear.

Fear → Inaction: Perhaps most significantly, fear inhibits action. It creates a state of paralysis where we know what we should do but feel unable to do it. This is the infamous "knowing-doing gap" we'll explore more fully in the next chapter.

Inaction → Results: When fear prevents us from taking aligned action, we create results (or lack thereof) that confirm our original limiting identity. The wheel completes another turn, and fear strengthens its grip.

The insight here is crucial: fear is not merely an uncomfortable emotion to be managed; it's a pivotal force in the cycle of self-limitation. By addressing fear directly, we can create an intervention point that transforms the entire Identity Wheel [34].

The Fear Barrier: Understanding the Gateway to Growth

When we set out to create meaningful change in our lives, we inevitably encounter what my mentor Bob Proctor calls the "terror

Chapter 6: Beyond Fear –Reclaiming Your Power

barrier" which is a threshold of discomfort that stands between our current reality and our desired future. This concept has been transformative in my own journey and in the lives of countless others I've worked with.

The fear barrier emerges when our new, empowering thoughts begin to challenge our established identity and beliefs. This creates internal conflict, as the old programming fights to maintain its dominance. The resulting discomfort manifests as fear, often intense enough to send us retreating back to the safety of our comfort zone.

What makes the fear barrier so challenging is that it appears precisely when we're making progress. This fear confirms you're on the right path. The fear barrier is the guardian at the gateway to our growth, testing our commitment to change.

Understanding the four stages of transformation can help us recognise and navigate the fear barrier more effectively:

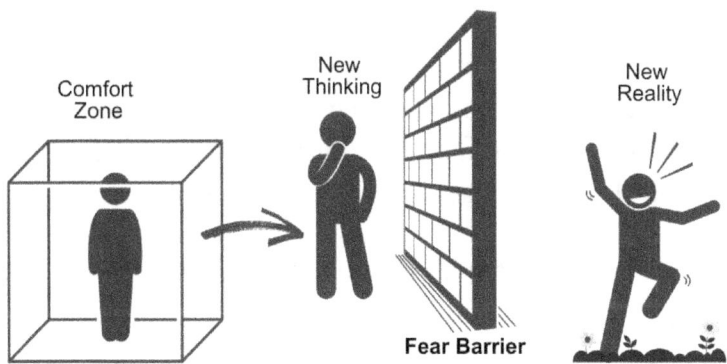

1. **Current State**: This is our comfort zone, where our thoughts, identity, actions and results are all aligned, creating a stable (if limiting) system.
2. **New Thinking**: We begin entertaining new possibilities, imagining a different future and nurturing empowering thoughts. This feels good and exciting. but it's still safely in the realm of imagination.
3. **Fear Barrier**: As we take the first steps towards actualising our new thinking, we encounter the fear barrier. This is where our subconscious programming activates fear to pull us back to safety. It's the moment of truth in our transformation journey. This internal conflict is where most people give up as the fear barrier is like a bungee cord tied around them, constantly trying to pull them back to the safety of the familiar.
4. **New Reality**: Beyond the fear barrier lies our new way of being, where our expanded identity, empowering thoughts, positive emotions and aligned actions create the results we desire.

Most people cycle between stages 1 and 2 throughout their lives, dreaming of change but retreating when they hit the fear barrier. The most successful among us aren't those who never feel fear, they're those who've learned to recognise the fear barrier as a signpost of growth and developed strategies to move through it.

The Three Faces of Fear: Recognising What Holds You Back

To transform your relationship with fear, it's essential to recognise its primary manifestations. When we examine fear closely, we discover that it typically presents in three fundamental forms:

Chapter 6: Beyond Fear –Reclaiming Your Power

1. Fear of Inadequacy: "I'm not enough"

This fear stems from the belief that we lack what it takes to succeed, whether in terms of intelligence, talent, skill, education, connections or some other perceived essential quality. It manifests as impostor syndrome, perfectionism and self-doubt.

The voice of inadequacy says: "Who am I to do this? I don't have what it takes. I'll be exposed as a fraud. I need more preparation, more credentials, more experience before I can take this step." [35]

2. Fear of Rejection: "I won't be accepted"

This fear centres on the social consequences of our actions and choices. It's rooted in our deep-seated need for belonging and acceptance by others. It manifests as people-pleasing, conformity and reluctance to express our authentic selves.

The voice of rejection says: "What will people think? They'll judge me. I'll lose their approval. I'll be criticised, ridiculed or excluded if I do this."

3. Fear of Failure: "I won't succeed"

This fear focuses on the outcome of our efforts. It's concerned with the possibility that our actions won't produce the desired results or meet our expectations. It manifests as procrastination, hesitation and abandoning projects before completion.

The voice of failure says: "What if it doesn't work? What if I waste my time and energy? What if I try my best and still fall short? Better not to try than to try and fail." [36]

These three fears aren't separate entities but interconnected aspects of our relationship with fear. They overlap and reinforce each other, creating a complex web that can feel impossible to untangle.

The power of naming these fears comes in recognising that they're not facts but instead interpretations based on limiting beliefs and past experiences. When we identify which face of fear is present in a particular situation, we can address it directly rather than being controlled by its invisible influence.

Procrastination and Self-Sabotage: Fear in Disguise

Among the most common and insidious manifestations of fear are procrastination and self-sabotage. These behaviours often appear as simple character flaws or bad habits, but they're typically sophisticated fear-management strategies that operate below our conscious awareness. It took me until my early thirties to realise how much self-sabotage had held me back from achieving any form of noticeable success [37].

Procrastination (the act of delaying important tasks despite negative consequences) is rarely about laziness. Instead, it's usually a fear-management tactic designed to protect us from potential discomfort, failure or negative judgement. By putting off a challenging task, we temporarily escape the anxiety associated with it and gain momentary relief. This reinforces the behaviour, creating a vicious cycle that's difficult to break.

I consistently delayed working on this book despite my genuine passion for the project. When I explored the underlying fears driving my procrastination, I discovered it wasn't about laziness

Chapter 6: Beyond Fear –Reclaiming Your Power

but about protecting my identity and self-image. "If I never finish the book," I realised, "I never have to face the possibility that it might be rejected or criticised. I get to keep my dream of being a writer without risking failure." I also found myself stuck in an endless loop of telling myself, "I don't know where to start", which provided a convenient excuse to never actually begin writing at all.

Self-sabotage operates in a similar fashion but goes a step further. It involves actively undermining our own success despite consciously wanting positive outcomes. This paradoxical behaviour makes sense when we recognise that achieving success often triggers fear: Fear of increased responsibility, fear of visibility, fear of not sustaining the achievement or even fear that success will change our relationships with others.

The journey from emotional paralysis to empowered action often requires us to act with fear rather than waiting for it to subside. This approach of taking action despite emotional resistance is beautifully demonstrated by Amara's artistic breakthrough.

The paintings lined Amara's apartment walls like beautiful prisoners – bold, raw canvases that captured something profound about human struggle and hope. Each piece represented months of work, but they'd never seen daylight beyond her cramped studio. The thought of strangers viewing her art triggered a panic response so severe she'd sometimes spend entire nights pacing her apartment.

"They're too personal," she'd whisper to her reflection. "Too weird. People will think I'm pretentious." The fear had paralysed her for three years, leaving enough completed work for six exhibitions gathering dust in her spare room.

The Identity Wheel

The breaking point came at her sister's birthday party. A guest noticed sketches on Amara's refrigerator and asked if she was an artist. "Oh no," Amara laughed nervously, "I just mess around with paints. It's nothing serious." Her sister Zara, who'd watched this self-sabotage for years, finally exploded: "Nothing serious? Are you insane? You've been creating masterpieces and treating them like embarrassing secrets!"

That night, Zara saw the paintings properly for the first time. She stood before a swirling canvas of blues and greys, Amara's visual representation of depression lifting, with tears streaming down her face. "People need to see these," she whispered. "You're depriving the world."

Amara started impossibly small: one painting shared with a trusted friend. The friend's reaction was immediate and emotional: "This is exactly how I felt after my mother died. How did you capture that?" That single validation cracked something open. A small café showing followed, then collaborative exhibitions, each step feeling terrifying yet increasingly natural.

Six months later, at her first solo exhibition opening, Amara watched a stranger stand before her depression painting for ten full minutes, clearly moved. The fear hadn't disappeared, it had transformed from prison guard to advisor, present but no longer in control.

Amara's experience illustrates a crucial truth: the more you take action despite fear and resistance, the more you train your subconscious to understand that these feelings aren't emergencies to be avoided but simply normal emotional weather to be experienced while continuing forward.

Chapter 6: Beyond Fear –Reclaiming Your Power

These behaviours can also stem from a deeper fear that psychologists call "fear of success". This seemingly contradictory phenomenon occurs when achieving our goals threatens our current identity or challenges our subconscious beliefs about what we deserve. It's particularly common among people from backgrounds where success was rare or viewed with suspicion [38].

The most effective approach to addressing procrastination and self-sabotage is to recognise them not as personal failings but as fear-based protective mechanisms. When you notice these patterns emerging, pause and ask yourself:

- What am I actually afraid of in this situation?
- What is this behaviour protecting me from experiencing?
- What identity or belief might I be trying to preserve?
- What would be possible if I moved forward despite this fear?

By bringing these subconscious fears into the light of conscious awareness, you can begin to address the root cause rather than battling the symptoms. This is the first step towards transforming these limiting patterns into opportunities for growth and authentic self-expression.

Fear versus Intuition: Discerning the Difference

One of the most common questions I hear is, "How do I know whether I'm feeling fear or intuition?" This distinction is crucial because fear holds us back from growth, while intuition guides us towards our highest good, yet both can generate similar sensations of caution or hesitation [39].

Here are several key distinctions to help you discern between fear and intuition:

1. **Quality of Sensation**: Fear typically creates constriction, tightness or heaviness in the body. It accelerates heart rate and can trigger shallow breathing. Intuition, by contrast, often manifests as a calm knowing, a quiet certainty or a neutral awareness, even when delivering challenging guidance.
2. **Relationship to Time**: Fear is usually fixated on the future, catastrophising about what might happen. Intuition tends to be grounded in the present moment, a clear perception of what is happening now and what it means.
3. **Complexity versus Simplicity**: Fear generates a whirlwind of thoughts, worries and scenarios. It's verbose and dramatic. Intuition is typically simple, quiet and straightforward, a clear signal amid the noise.
4. **Energy Level**: Fear drains your energy, leaving you feeling depleted and exhausted. Intuition, even when pointing towards difficult truths, tends to bring clarity and a sense of relief or resolution.
5. **Growth Orientation**: Fear almost always directs you away from growth and back towards safety and the familiar. Intuition, while sometimes cautioning against particular paths, ultimately guides you towards your highest development and authentic expression.

I'll never forget the example of a talented artist who had abandoned her creative work for a "practical" corporate career. She was considering returning to her art but felt tremendous hesitation. "I don't know if this feeling is fear or my intuition telling me it's a bad idea," she confided.

When exploring this sensation, several key distinctions emerged: the hesitation felt tight and anxious (fear), generated endless "what if" scenarios about financial disaster (future-focused fear), created mental chaos rather than clarity (complex fear), left her feeling drained rather than resolved (energy-depleting fear), and ultimately directed her away from what she knew was her path of growth.

Once she recognised she was dealing with fear rather than intuition, she could address it directly and make choices from a place of clarity rather than confusion.

Five Strategies for Moving Beyond Fear

Now that we understand the nature of fear, how it operates within the Identity Wheel and how to recognise its various manifestations, let's explore practical strategies for transforming our relationship with fear.

1. Conscious Fear Inventory

The first step in transforming your relationship with fear is bringing it into conscious awareness. Many of our fears operate below the surface, influencing our choices without our knowledge. A conscious fear inventory helps you identify and name the specific fears that are limiting your growth.

Take out your journal and divide a page into three columns labelled "Situation", "Fear" and "Reality Check". In the first column, list circumstances where you feel held back or resistant to change.

In the second column, identify which specific fear is present (inadequacy, rejection, failure or a combination). In the third column, challenge the fear with questions like:

- What evidence suggests this fear is justified?
- What evidence contradicts this fear?
- What's the worst that could realistically happen?
- How would I handle that worst-case scenario?
- What's the cost of allowing this fear to limit me?

This exercise doesn't eliminate fear, but it transforms it from an invisible force controlling you to a visible thought pattern you can work with consciously.

2. The Fear Ladder Technique

The fear ladder is a gradual exposure approach that helps you build confidence by tackling fears in manageable increments. This technique is based on the psychological principle that controlled exposure to feared situations, in a stepped approach, reduces the fear response over time.

To create your fear ladder:

1. Identify a specific fear that's holding you back
2. Break down the fear into 5–10 steps of increasing intensity
3. Start with the least intimidating step and practise until your fear subsides
4. Gradually work your way up to more challenging steps

For example, if you fear public speaking, your ladder might include recording yourself speaking alone, speaking to one supportive friend, speaking in a small group of trusted colleagues and so on, working up to presenting to a large audience.

The key is consistent practice at each level until that step no longer triggers significant fear before moving to the next level. This creates a series of small wins that transform your relationship with the fear over time.

3. Embodied Courage Practices

Fear is not merely a mental phenomenon; it lives in the body as well. Embodied courage practices work with the physical manifestations of fear to create transformation.

The "courage pose" is particularly effective: Stand with your feet hip-width apart, shoulders back, chest open, head held high, and arms either at your sides or in a "V" above your head. Hold this posture for two minutes while breathing deeply.

Research by social psychologist Amy Cuddy has shown that adopting powerful postures like this actually changes your physiology, reducing stress hormones and increasing testosterone, which is associated with confidence. This creates a positive feedback loop between your body and mind [40].

A perfect example of this can be seen with Dr Amelia Shepherd from Grey's Anatomy, who frequently adopts power poses throughout the TV show. Before difficult surgeries or challenging conversations, she can often be seen standing with her hands on her hips in a superhero stance. This physical ritual helps her channel confidence when facing high-pressure neurosurgeries or personal challenges, demonstrating how embodying confidence physically can help manifest it mentally, especially in high-stakes situations.

Combine this practice with conscious breathing, particularly box breathing, where you inhale for a count of four, hold for four, exhale for four, and hold for four, repeating the cycle several times. This activates your parasympathetic nervous system, countering the fight-or-flight response that fear triggers.

These embodied practices are particularly valuable in moments when fear arises unexpectedly, providing immediate tools to shift your state.

4. Reframing Fear as Excitement

One of the most fascinating discoveries in the science of emotions is that the physiological signatures of fear and excitement are nearly identical. Both involve elevated heart rate, increased breathing, heightened alertness and surges of adrenaline. The primary difference is the cognitive label we attach to these sensations.

Harvard psychologist Alison Wood Brooks has shown that simply relabelling anxiety as excitement significantly improves performance in stressful situations. When participants in her studies said "I am excited" out loud before challenging tasks, they performed better than those who tried to calm themselves or who did nothing to manage their emotions [41].

This "anxiety reappraisal" works because it transforms a threat mindset (fear) into an opportunity mindset (excitement) without

Chapter 6: Beyond Fear –Reclaiming Your Power

requiring you to suppress the physiological arousal you're experiencing, which is virtually impossible in the moment anyway.

When I go to speak, I can often feel fear kicking in, but once I recognise it, I tell myself this feeling is my body telling me "I'm going to add some real value today" and "This feeling means something good is going to happen". I couple this with box breathing to further harness the energy.

The next time you feel fear arising, try saying aloud: "I'm not afraid; I'm excited. This feeling is my body preparing for optimal performance". This simple shift can transform fear from an obstacle into fuel for action.

5. The Future Self Dialogue

This powerful approach leverages your connection with your future self – the person you're becoming through this transformational journey.

Find a quiet space where you won't be interrupted. Close your eyes and visualise meeting your future self who has already moved beyond the fear that currently limits you. This is the version of you who has crossed the fear barrier and is living in your desired reality.

In your imagination, ask your future self:

- How did you overcome the fear I'm experiencing?
- What perspective or understanding made the difference?
- What would you say to me now as I face this challenge?

The Identity Wheel

Then listen for the response, allowing it to emerge naturally without forcing it.

This exercise harnesses the power of your imagination to access wisdom that already exists within you but is currently obscured by fear. It creates an emotional connection with your future self that can provide motivation and guidance when fear arises.

The Freedom Beyond Fear: What Becomes Possible

As we conclude this exploration of fear, let's consider what becomes possible when you develop mastery in this domain. Moving beyond fear doesn't mean you'll never feel afraid again; it means you'll have transformed your relationship with fear so that it no longer controls your choices and limits your potential.

Returning to Marianne Williamson's powerful quote used in Coach Carter: "As we are liberated from our own fear, our presence automatically liberates others." Your liberation creates a ripple effect - as you step into freedom, you give others permission to claim theirs.

When you move beyond fear, you experience:

Authentic Self-Expression: Rather than conforming to others' expectations or hiding aspects of yourself to avoid rejection, you express your authentic essence freely. Your words, actions and creative expressions become aligned with your true self rather than shaped by fear of judgement.

Expanded Capacity for Risk: You develop the ability to take calculated risks that lead to growth, not recklessly but with clear-eyed assessment of both potential rewards and potential challenges. You no longer automatically choose the safe option by default.

Resilience in Uncertainty: Life is inherently uncertain, and beyond fear lies the capacity to navigate uncertainty with grace rather than resist it with anxiety. You develop trust in your ability to handle whatever arises, even when you can't predict or control the outcome.

Accelerated Growth: As the Identity Wheel spins in a positive direction, free from the friction of fear, your rate of personal and professional growth accelerates dramatically. You move more quickly through learning curves that previously might have taken years to navigate.

Expanded Impact: Perhaps most significantly, as you overcome your own fears, you naturally inspire and empower others to do the same. Your example creates a ripple effect, touching lives beyond your immediate circle and contributing to positive change in the wider world.

Moving beyond fear is not a destination but an ongoing journey, one that becomes increasingly rewarding as you develop greater skill at recognising and transforming fear when it arises. Each time you consciously choose growth over safety, action over paralysis and authentic expression over conformity, you strengthen neural pathways that make this choice easier in the future.

Looking Ahead

Fear doesn't disappear through avoidance; it transforms through understanding. When you stop running from it and start listening to it, fear becomes less of a barrier and more of a compass, pointing towards the exact growth your soul is ready for.

Begin noticing when fear whispers to you, noticing what it says, when it shows up and how it subtly shapes your decisions. Awareness is the first crack in fear's illusion of control.

In the next chapter, we'll shift from inner reflection to external creation. You'll learn how to close the gap between what you *know* and what you *do* and how to move with courage, even when fear still lingers in the room.

Because transformation doesn't wait for fear to vanish. It happens when you act anyway.

Chapter 6: Beyond Fear – Reclaiming Your Power

Chapter Summary

Fear appears as guardian and prison guard, evolving from physical survival mechanisms to psychological, social and existential concerns.

Our deepest fear often isn't inadequacy but our own power beyond measure.

Fear influences every element of the Identity Wheel, from identity to results.

The fear barrier emerges when new thoughts challenge established identity, creating internal conflict.

Fear manifests in three primary forms: fear of inadequacy, fear of rejection and fear of failure.

Procrastination and self-sabotage operate as sophisticated fear management strategies.

Distinguishing fear from intuition involves examining quality of sensation, relationship to time, complexity, energy level and growth orientation.

Five strategies for moving beyond fear: Conscious Fear Inventory, Fear Ladder Technique, Embodied Courage Practices, Reframing Fear as Excitement, and Future Self Dialogue.

REFLECTION QUESTIONS

1. What specific fears have most significantly limited your growth? Which face of fear (inadequacy, rejection, failure) is most active in your life?
2. How might your life be different if you viewed fear as a signpost of growth rather than a warning to retreat?
3. Can you identify a situation where what you initially perceived as fear might actually have been intuition? What was different about this experience?

PRACTICAL EXERCISES

1. Fear Inventory

- Create three columns: "Fear of Inadequacy" "Fear of Rejection" and "Fear of Failure"
- Under each heading, list situations where this type of fear arises for you
- Circle the three most significant fears that limit your growth
- For each circled fear, ask:
    - What's the worst that could realistically happen?
    - Could I handle that outcome if it occurred?
    - What might I gain by moving forward despite this fear?

2. Fear as Growth Compass

- Identify something you want but have avoided due to fear
- Ask yourself:
    - What scares me most about this?

- o What might this fear be trying to teach me?
        - o What strength or capability might I develop by facing this?
    - Identify one small action you could take towards this desired outcome

3. Fear vs. Intuition Discernment

- Recall two situations:
    - o One where hesitation was driven by fear
    - o One where hesitation was driven by intuition
- For each situation, note:
    - o The quality of the sensation (constricting vs. neutral)
    - o The focus (future possibilities vs. present reality)
    - o The energy level (draining vs. clarifying)
    - o The outcome of following or ignoring the feeling
- Use these insights to create your personal criteria for distinguishing fear from intuition

The Identity Wheel

Chapter 7: Action – Bridging the Knowing-Doing Gap

In the previous chapters, we've explored how the Identity Wheel illustrates the cyclical nature of our identity, thoughts, emotions, actions and results. We've examined the architecture of the mind that powers this wheel, delved into our core identity statements, explored the power of our thoughts and beliefs and learned how to master our emotional landscape. Now, we turn our attention to what is perhaps the most pivotal element of personal transformation: action.

Action is where the intangible becomes tangible, where internal shifts in identity, thought and emotion manifest as visible changes in your external reality. It's the bridge between knowing and doing, between potential and achievement, between who you are now and who you're capable of becoming.

Yet for many, this bridge remains uncrossed. They possess the knowledge, harbour the right intentions, even feel the motivation but still struggle to take consistent action towards their goals. This "knowing-doing gap" represents one of the most significant obstacles to personal growth and success. In this chapter, we'll explore why this gap exists and, more importantly, how to bridge it effectively.

The Knowing-Doing Gap Explained

Knowledge is abundant in our information-rich world. With a few keystrokes, you can access more information on any topic than previous generations could find in entire libraries. You have more information available to you on your phone than any king, queen or emperor in history. Let that sink in. Yet despite this wealth of knowledge, many people find themselves stuck in patterns of inaction or ineffective action.

The knowing-doing gap describes that puzzling space between what we know we should do and what we actually do. It's why someone might read dozens of books on fitness while remaining sedentary, or study financial planning while continuing to accumulate debt or understand the principles of healthy relationships while repeating the same destructive patterns [42].

From an early age, our education is set up to get us to know things, to know more, know more, know more. We walk around collecting knowledge, still not living the life that we want. We're constantly

Chapter 7: Action – Bridging the Knowing-Doing Gap

seeking more information because we think that's the solution. The real solution? Apply what you already know.

If I asked you, "Do you know how to be 1% healthier?" the answer would be yes. If I asked, "Do you know how to improve your relationships by 1%?" the answer would be yes. If I asked, "Do you know how to improve your work by 1%?" once again, the answer would be yes. We know what to do. We just don't actually do it.

Why does this gap exist? The answer lies in the structure of our mind and the power of our subconscious programming. As we learned in previous chapters – what we know is conscious. What we do is largely subconscious. These are two separate parts of us, operating under different rules. This is why we struggle so much. We get so frustrated because we know we can do better. We want to do better. But we don't stop to work on the subconscious programmes that are causing the issue.

Our mental programmes are responsible for our actions and consequently our results. These programmes create the prism through which we view and make sense of the world around us. When information is presented to your mind, your mind runs through all of the things it already knows about that piece of information based on your past experiences. It figures out where this new information fits in with the bigger picture and decides if the information is good or bad, desirable or undesirable, positive or negative.

But these programmes aren't positive or negative; they just are. In certain areas of your life, you're getting fantastic results because you have very good, positive programmes running. We're concerned with the ones that are actually holding us back and stopping us from reaching our full potential.

The problem is that we try to change the behaviour (the action) without addressing the root cause of the behaviour: the subconscious programmes. So the change never lasts. We can consciously commit to change, saying to ourselves: "I'm going to exercise every day" or "I'm going to save money this month", but what happens as soon as we stop consciously thinking about it? We slip back into our old habits and routines. That is your programmes at work.

To bridge the knowing-doing gap, we must address both levels of mind: the conscious mind that knows what to do and the subconscious mind that actually drives our actions.

The Paralysis of Overthinking

One of the most common obstacles to action is overthinking. In our quest to make perfect decisions, we can become trapped in analysis paralysis, that state where the fear of making the wrong choice prevents us from making any choice at all.

Hyder, a talented marketing professional, found himself stuck in this pattern. He had dreams of starting his own agency but couldn't seem to take the first step. "I spent months researching the market, analysing competitors and refining my business plan," he shared. "But I kept finding new things to consider, new angles to explore. It was never quite ready to launch." What Hyder didn't realise was that his perfectionism wasn't serving him; it was actually a sophisticated form of procrastination, a way to avoid the discomfort of putting himself out there.

Chapter 7: Action – Bridging the Knowing-Doing Gap

Perfectionism often masks a deeper fear: the fear of being judged, the fear of failing or even the fear of succeeding. By setting impossibly high standards, perfectionists create a safety net, because if they never finish something, they never have to face criticism or disappointment. The irony, of course, is that this "safety" comes at the cost of never experiencing growth or achievement.

The solution to overthinking isn't less thinking – it's balanced thinking followed by decisive action. It's acknowledging that imperfect action is almost always better than perfect inaction.

When Hyder finally decided to launch his business with what he called a "minimum viable business," something remarkable happened. "The feedback I got from those first few clients shaped my services and approach in ways I never could have predicted from behind my desk," he recalled. "All those months of planning couldn't compare to a week of actually working with real clients."

The lesson is clear: thinking has its place in planning and strategy, but it must eventually yield to action. As the ancient Chinese proverb says, "Talk doesn't cook rice."

The Comfort Zone Trap

Another major obstacle to bridging the knowing-doing gap is our natural tendency to seek comfort and avoid discomfort. Your comfort zone is a state where things feel familiar, safe and certain. It's where you know what to expect and feel confident in your ability to handle the situations you encounter.

While there's nothing inherently wrong with comfort, growth happens at the edge of discomfort. Every significant achievement in your life likely required you to step beyond what felt safe and familiar.

The comfort zone trap works like this: you set a goal that genuinely excites you. You make plans, gather information and feel motivated to begin. But as soon as you take the first steps towards that goal, you encounter resistance, that internal discomfort in the form of fear, doubt or uncertainty (as we learned in the last chapter). Rather than pushing through this discomfort, you retreat to the safety of your comfort zone, where those uncomfortable feelings subside.

Over time, this pattern reinforces itself. Your brain learns that stepping outside your comfort zone leads to discomfort, while retreating to familiar territory brings relief. This creates a powerful unconscious bias towards inaction when faced with new challenges.

Emily, a corporate lawyer, had dreamed of transitioning to environmental law for years. "I had all the knowledge: I'd taken courses, read books, even shadowed an environmental lawyer for a day," she explained. "But every time I came close to making the switch, I'd find reasons to delay: 'I should build my network more' or 'I need one more certification.'" What Emily eventually realised was that her hesitation wasn't about insufficient preparation; it was about avoiding the discomfort of being a beginner again after years of expertise in her current field.

Breaking free from the comfort zone trap requires recognising that discomfort is not your enemy, it's a signpost pointing towards growth. Rather than avoiding discomfort, we can learn to embrace it as a necessary companion on the path to achievement.

Emily finally made the leap when she reframed her thinking: "Instead of seeing discomfort as a warning sign, I started seeing it as confirmation that I was growing. That complete shift in perspective made all the difference."

The Power of Disciplined Action

Now that we understand some of the major obstacles to action, let's explore what makes action effective. Not all action is created equal. Scattered, inconsistent efforts rarely produce meaningful results. The kind of action that transforms lives is disciplined, consistent and aligned with your deeper goals and values.

Discipline is often misunderstood. Many see it as a form of punishment or restriction, as something to be endured rather than embraced. But true discipline is actually a pathway to freedom. When you are disciplined, you gain control over your life rather than being controlled by momentary impulses or external pressures.

Think of discipline as doing what needs to be done, even when you don't feel like doing it. This definition, shared by my mentor Andy Frisella, perfectly captures the transformative power that develops when we cultivate this trait. Discipline is the crucial bridge that spans the gap between your intentions and your actions, between your knowledge and your results. It's this consistent commitment to action (regardless of momentary feelings) that ultimately transforms potential into achievement [43].

Katie, who we met earlier in chapter 5, struggled for years to finish her novel before discovering the transformative power of discipline. "I used to write only when inspiration struck, which might be once a week or once a month," she shared. "I'd have these brilliant creative bursts followed by weeks of nothing." Katie's breakthrough came when she established a daily writing practice of just 30 minutes, regardless of whether she felt inspired.

"Some days, those 30 minutes were pure torture," she admitted. "I'd stare at the blank page, write a sentence, delete it, check the clock, it was agonising. But I showed up anyway." Over time, Katie noticed something shifting. "The muse started showing up more reliably when she knew I'd be at my desk, ready to work. The days of forced writing became less frequent, and my overall output quadrupled."

Katie's experience illustrates a fundamental truth: discipline creates the conditions for success. By showing up consistently, you train both your conscious and subconscious mind to align with your goals.

The beauty of discipline is that it becomes easier over time. What initially requires conscious effort eventually becomes automatic, a habit that requires little willpower to maintain. This is the power of disciplined action: it compounds, becoming both more effective and less effortful the longer you practise it.

Discipline isn't punishment you inflict on yourself; it's freedom you give to yourself.

Chapter 7: Action – Bridging the Knowing-Doing Gap

Creating Habits That Drive Success

Habits are the building blocks of action. While disciplined action might get you started, habits are what sustain your progress over the long term. A habit is simply a behaviour that has become so automatic that you do it with minimal conscious thought or effort.

The power of habits lies in their efficiency. When something becomes habitual, it bypasses the knowing-doing gap entirely. You don't need to decide to do it; you just do it. This conserves your mental energy for other tasks that do require conscious decision-making [44].

To create habits that drive success, it's important to understand how habits form and function. James Clear, in his influential book "Atomic Habits", outlines the four-stage habit loop that governs all habitual behaviour:

1. **Cue**: The trigger that initiates the behaviour.
2. **Craving**: The motivational force behind the behaviour.
3. **Response**: The actual habit or behaviour itself.
4. **Reward**: The benefit you gain from the behaviour.

This four-step process forms what behavioural scientists call the "habit loop". By understanding and manipulating this loop, as Clear demonstrates, you can create new habits that support your goals and break old habits that hinder them [45].

The key to habit formation is consistency, especially in the early stages. Research suggests that it takes anywhere from 18 to 254 days to form a new habit, with an average of about 66 days. During this formation period, conscious effort and intention are required.

But once the habit is established, it operates largely on autopilot, free from the constraints of the knowing-doing gap [46].

When designing new habits, start small. Many people fail in habit formation because they try to change too much too quickly. A small habit that you actually perform consistently is far more powerful than an ambitious habit that quickly falls by the wayside.

For instance, if your goal is to exercise regularly then starting with a commitment to walk for five minutes each day is more likely to succeed than planning hour-long gym sessions five times a week. Once the five-minute walk becomes habitual, you can gradually expand it.

The Power List: A Tool for Daily Success

One of the most effective tools for bridging the knowing-doing gap is what I call the Power List. Unlike a traditional to-do list, which can become an overwhelming catalogue of tasks, the Power List is a focused action plan for daily success.

The Power List consists of just **five key actions** that you commit to completing each day. These aren't just any tasks; they're the specific actions that will move you closer to your most important goals. By limiting the list to five items, you make it manageable and increase the likelihood of completion.

This powerful concept was taught to me by my mentor Andy Frisella, who I mentioned earlier. This is his concept that I am sharing with you. His straightforward approach to daily achievement has transformed not only my life but the lives of

Chapter 7: Action – Bridging the Knowing-Doing Gap

thousands of his followers. Here's how to create an effective Power List:

1. **Choose actions, not outcomes**: Focus on behaviours within your control, not results that depend on external factors. For example, "Contact five potential clients" rather than "Make two sales".
2. **Prioritise impact**: Select actions that will have the greatest positive impact on your long-term goals. Ask yourself, "If I could only accomplish five things today, which would move me furthest towards my vision?"
3. **Be specific**: Define exactly what completing each action entails. Rather than "Work on project", specify "Complete section 3 of the project report".
4. **Ensure accountability**: Make your actions measurable so you can clearly determine whether you've completed them.
5. **Commit to completion**: The Power List isn't a suggestion – it's a commitment. These five actions take priority over other tasks that may arise throughout the day.

The power of this approach lies in its simplicity and focus. By consistently completing these high-impact actions, you create momentum towards your goals and train your subconscious mind to align with your conscious intentions.

Thomas, a business owner struggling with consistent growth, used the Power List with remarkable results. "Before, I was busy all day but didn't see much progress," he explained. "I'd react to whatever came up: emails, phone calls, staff issues, and end the day exhausted but with nothing substantial accomplished."

The Identity Wheel

After adopting the Power List, Thomas began each day by identifying his five high-impact actions. "It completely changed my approach. Instead of reacting, I was proactive. Even on chaotic days, I'd ensure those five key actions were completed." Within three months, Thomas had doubled his client base and increased revenue by 35%, all while working fewer hours.

What makes the Power List so effective is that it bridges the knowing-doing gap by focusing your energy on a small number of consequential actions. It transforms vague good intentions into specific, achievable commitments. And when you consistently follow through on these commitments, you build self-trust and confidence, further narrowing the gap between knowing and doing.

Power List

The 5 key actions I commit to completing today that will move me closer to my goal are:

1.
2.
3.
4.
5.

Notes

Chapter 7: Action – Bridging the Knowing-Doing Gap

Overcoming Fear and Resistance

Even with tools like the Power List, you'll inevitably encounter fear and resistance on your journey. These internal obstacles can be powerful enough to halt even the most determined individual if not properly addressed.

As we discussed in the previous chapter, fear manifests in many forms: fear of failure, fear of success, fear of rejection, fear of the unknown. At its core, fear is your brain's way of trying to protect you from perceived threats. While this mechanism is valuable in genuinely dangerous situations, it often misidentifies growth opportunities as threats.

Resistance, a concept popularised by author Steven Pressfield, is that internal force that arises whenever you attempt to do anything important or meaningful. It's the voice that says, "I'll start tomorrow" or "I'm not ready yet" or "This isn't the right time".

Both fear and resistance are natural responses to stepping beyond your comfort zone. The key is not to eliminate them (that's rarely possible) but to act despite their presence.

Rachael, a talented corporate trainer, experienced paralysing fear whenever she attempted to deliver workshops publicly. "I'd develop these training programmes that I was proud of, but the thought of standing in front of a room full of professionals made me physically ill," she recounted. "I'd find endless reasons to delay: the content wasn't polished enough, I needed more case studies, the timing wasn't right."

Rachael's breakthrough came when she learned to recognise fear and resistance as normal companions on the professional journey rather than indicators that something was wrong. "I started saying to myself, 'Oh, there's that fear again. It always shows up when I'm about to do something important.' Just that recognition took away some of its power."

She developed a simple process for moving forward despite fear:

Acknowledge: "I notice I'm feeling afraid right now."

Validate: "It's natural to feel fear when doing something new or meaningful."

Refocus: "What's one small action I can take right now, even with the fear present?"

This process allowed Rachael to take incremental steps forward without requiring the fear to disappear first. She began by delivering her programme to a trusted colleague, then to a small team, then at a collaborative conference, and finally running her own public workshop.

"The fear never completely went away," she admitted, "but it changed from a paralysing force to more of a background hum. And sometimes, it even feels like useful energy now."

This approach of acting with fear rather than waiting for it to subside is essential for bridging the knowing-doing gap. The more you take action despite fear and resistance, the more you train your subconscious to understand that these feelings aren't emergencies to be avoided but simply normal emotional weather to be experienced while continuing forward.

Chapter 7: Action – Bridging the Knowing-Doing Gap

Setting Boundaries to Protect Your Energy

One often overlooked aspect of effective action is the protection of your energy and focus. In our hyperconnected world, distractions and demands on your time and attention are constant. Without clear boundaries, these external forces can easily derail even the most disciplined action plan.

Boundaries are not walls to keep people out but rather bridges that allow the right people in and keep the wrong people out. They define what is acceptable to you and what isn't, creating a protected space where your most important work can flourish [47].

The power of boundaries becomes immediately apparent when we see how their absence can sabotage even the most dedicated efforts. This was precisely Chen's challenge.

Chen's phone buzzed for the fourth time in seven minutes. Another "urgent" email marked high priority. It was 7:42 AM, and his day was already spiralling before he'd finished his coffee. As the "go-to guy" at his software company, Chen had built his reputation on instant responses and unwavering availability. His colleagues joked that he never slept. His manager praised his "exceptional responsiveness".

But Chen was drowning.

Despite 60-hour weeks and constant accessibility, his strategic projects (the ones that could showcase leadership potential) sat perpetually on the back burner while he handled an endless stream of "emergencies" that often proved trivial. His girlfriend

Mei had started making pointed comments: "You're never really here. Even during dinner, you're waiting for the next crisis."

She was right. Chen lived in a state of hypervigilance, his nervous system always on high alert. He'd lost the ability to focus deeply because every notification triggered his rescue response.

The breaking point came during his annual review. His manager David delivered feedback that felt like a gut punch: "Chen, you're incredibly hardworking, but I'm concerned about your strategic impact. You're so busy putting out fires that you're not building anything meaningful. For your next promotion, we need to see you taking ownership of bigger initiatives."

Chen left that meeting devastated and confused. He worked harder than anyone else. How could he possibly do more? That weekend, feeling desperate, he attended a time management workshop where the facilitator asked a simple question that changed everything: "What would happen if you weren't available for every small emergency? Would the company collapse, or would people find other solutions?"

The truth was uncomfortable: his constant availability had trained others to depend on him for problems they could solve themselves. He was enabling learned helplessness while sabotaging his own strategic work. Chen implemented radical boundaries: two hours each morning blocked for deep work, email checks at specific intervals only and clear expectations about response times.

The transformation was remarkable. Not only did fewer "emergencies" arise, because people started solving problems independently, but Chen finally had space for the strategic thinking that earned him a promotion six months later.

Chen's transformation illustrates a fundamental principle: boundaries aren't selfish; they're strategic. By protecting your energy and focus, you ensure that your actions are aligned with your highest priorities rather than scattered across whatever demands arise. This alignment is essential for bridging the knowing-doing gap effectively.

Remember that boundaries require both establishment and enforcement. Many people set boundaries but fail to defend them when they're tested. This undermines the entire system. When you set a boundary, be prepared to uphold it consistently, even when it's uncomfortable to do so.

Building Momentum Through Daily Wins

Success rarely comes from a single monumental action but rather from the accumulation of small, consistent actions over time. This principle lies at the heart of building momentum, creating a forward force that makes continued action easier and more natural.

The concept is simple: win the day, then make a habit of winning the day. Every single one of you can win the next 24 hours. And when you win one day, you build the confidence to win the next. This process of stacking daily wins creates powerful momentum towards your larger goals.

What constitutes a "win"? It's the completion of your Power List: those five key actions that move you towards your most important objectives. When you consistently complete these actions, you're not just making progress; you're training your subconscious mind to align with your conscious intentions.

Mathematically, if you win four out of seven days in a week, you've won the week. When you win the weeks, you win the months. When you win the months, you win the year. This is how you create lasting change and bridge the knowing-doing gap, one day at a time.

I struggled for years to complete this book or, if I'm honest, to even start it! It was only when I transformed my approach through this daily win philosophy that it all fell into place. Instead of thinking about finishing the entire book, which felt overwhelming, I discovered I just needed to focus on winning today by writing my 500 words, regardless of quality or inspiration.

This shift from focusing on the distant goal to concentrating on today's actions liberated me from the paralysis of perfectionism. Some days, those 500 words were brilliant, and some days they were awful. But they all counted as a win because the goal was the action, not the outcome.

Six months after adopting this approach, I had completed my manuscript, something I hadn't achieved in the previous three years of sporadic effort. This daily win philosophy became the foundation that helped me finally bring the book you're reading right now to completion.

The power of daily wins extends beyond the tangible progress they create. Each win strengthens your identity as someone who follows through, someone who takes action, someone who

Chapter 7: Action – Bridging the Knowing-Doing Gap

achieves. This identity shift is perhaps the most significant benefit, as it creates a new self-image that naturally generates aligned actions without constant conscious effort [48].

Remember, momentum works in both directions. Just as positive actions create forward momentum, inaction or negative actions create reverse momentum. This is why the guideline of "don't have two bad days in a row" is so important. If you miss your wins one day, double down on ensuring you win the next. This prevents the formation of negative momentum that can quickly undo your progress.

The Role of Environment in Supporting Action

Your physical and social environment plays a crucial role in either supporting or hindering your actions. Human beings are remarkably sensitive to environmental cues, often more than we realise. These cues can trigger habits, influence decisions and shape behaviour, all at a largely subconscious level.

Consider how your current environment might be affecting your actions. Are there visual reminders of your goals and priorities? Is your space arranged to make productive behaviours easier? Are the people around you supportive of your aspirations?

During my time as a personal trainer, I noticed that many of my clients struggled not with knowledge but with consistent doing. They knew exactly what to do, but their environments were working against them. Based on this insight, I developed an "environment audit" to help my clients align their surroundings with their fitness goals:

1. **Physical space**: I encouraged clients to arrange their environment to make desired behaviours easier and undesired behaviours harder. For those wanting to exercise in the morning, laying out workout clothes the night before made a tremendous difference. For those wanting to reduce unhealthy snacking, reorganising the kitchen to hide temptations and showcase nutritious options created automatic improvements.
2. **Visual cues**: I taught clients to surround themselves with reminders of their goals and values. This could be as simple as a vision board in their bedroom or as subtle as a meaningful quote on their water bottle, anything that would trigger their conscious mind to remember what they were working towards.
3. **Social environment**: We would assess whether the people they spent most time with supported or undermined their goals. I'd help them consider how they might increase time with positive influences and limit exposure to those who, often unintentionally, sabotaged their progress.
4. **Digital environment**: Together, we'd evaluate how their technology use affected their actions. Configuring notifications, setting screen time limits and rearranging app layouts helped support their priorities rather than distract from them.

One of my clients, Michelle, experienced a dramatic shift after implementing these environmental adjustments. "I'd been trying to build a morning workout habit for years without success," she shared during our review session. "But after rearranging my bedroom to create a dedicated exercise space and setting out my

Chapter 7: Action – Bridging the Knowing-Doing Gap

clothes each night, it suddenly became so much easier. It was like removing friction I didn't even know was there."

Your environment shapes your actions far more than willpower alone. By deliberately designing your surroundings to support your priorities, you create a powerful ally in bridging the knowing-doing gap.

The Ripple Effect of Action in the Identity Wheel

As we return to the Identity Wheel framework, we can now appreciate how action creates ripples that transform every aspect of the cycle. Action isn't just one component of the wheel; it's the catalyst that energises the entire system.

When you consistently take actions aligned with your desired identity and goals, you create results that confirm and strengthen that identity. This reinforced identity then generates thoughts and emotions that support even more effective action, creating a powerful upward spiral of growth and achievement.

Consider how this might play out in a practical example: Nick identifies as "not a public speaker" (identity). When asked to present at a conference, he thinks, "I'll probably make a fool of myself" (thoughts). These thoughts generate feelings of anxiety and inadequacy (emotions). However, unlike in our earlier examples, Nick decides to take action despite these emotions. Rather than being overwhelmed by it, he recognises it as natural nervous energy that he channels into thorough preparation. He thoroughly prepares, practises his presentation repeatedly and seeks feedback from trusted colleagues (actions).

His well-prepared presentation receives positive responses (results), which begin to challenge his original identity. This creates a crack in his limiting belief, allowing him to consider a new possibility: "Maybe I am capable of effective public speaking." This subtle identity shift influences his thoughts the next time a speaking opportunity arises, generating less anxiety and more confidence, which leads to even better preparation and delivery.

Over time, through consistent action, Nick's identity transforms from "I am not a public speaker" to "I am a confident and effective communicator". The wheel doesn't just turn; it evolves, creating a new set point for his experience.

This is the true power of action within the Identity Wheel, it doesn't merely create external results; it transforms your internal reality. Every aligned action you take, no matter how small, contributes to this transformation.

The Promise of Bridging the Gap

As we conclude this exploration of action and the knowing-doing gap, let's reflect on what becomes possible when you successfully bridge this divide. When knowledge and action align, you experience a profound sense of congruence because your outer life starts to reflect your inner values, goals and potential.

This alignment creates not just external success but also internal harmony. The frustration of knowing but not doing gives way to the satisfaction of living in accordance with your highest intentions. The energy previously consumed by internal conflict becomes available for creative expression and meaningful achievement.

Chapter 7: Action – Bridging the Knowing-Doing Gap

Moreover, as you consistently take aligned action, you develop an unshakable confidence in your ability to translate knowledge into results. This confidence isn't based on wishful thinking but on proven experience – you know you can do what you say you'll do because you've demonstrated it repeatedly.

Perhaps most importantly, bridging the knowing-doing gap allows you to access your full potential. Knowledge without action is like having a powerful car that never leaves the garage, impressive but ultimately purposeless. When you put that knowledge into action, you begin to experience the exhilaration of forward movement and the fulfilment of expressed potential.

Remember that bridging this gap is not a one-time achievement but an ongoing practice. There will always be new knowledge to implement, new challenges to overcome, new levels of alignment to achieve. Each day presents a fresh opportunity to win the day, to choose action over hesitation, to align your outer behaviour with your inner wisdom.

The Identity Wheel keeps turning, but with consistent, aligned action you increasingly determine its direction. Your actions are the rudder that steers the ship of your life. By mastering this crucial element of the wheel, you gain the power to navigate towards the life you truly desire to create.

Looking Ahead

Action is how intention becomes real. But what happens next (your results) are more than just outcomes. They're messages. Mirrors. Invitations.

The Identity Wheel

The moment you take a step, the universe responds. And how you interpret that response can either reinforce who you've always been or open the door to who you're becoming.

In the next chapter, we'll explore how results feed back into your identity, why self-fulfilling prophecies feel so hard to escape, and how to consciously shift the loop to work in your favour.

For now, notice where your actions are producing alignment, and where they aren't. Ask yourself: What feedback am I receiving? What's this teaching me about my beliefs, my habits and my current identity?

The wheel is always turning. The question is, are you turning it with intention? Or on autopilot?

Chapter 7: Action – Bridging the Knowing-Doing Gap

Chapter Summary

The knowing-doing gap describes the space between what we know we should do and what we actually do.

Subconscious programming drives actions despite conscious knowledge, creating this disconnect.

Overthinking creates paralysis when perfectionism disguises procrastination.

The comfort zone trap leads to retreating from growth-inducing discomfort.

Discipline means doing what needs to be done even when you don't feel like doing it.

The Power List of five key daily actions focuses energy on high-impact behaviours.

Habit formation follows the four-stage loop of cue, craving, response and reward.

Setting boundaries protects your energy and focus from constant distractions.

Daily wins create momentum that compounds over time, building confidence and aligned identity.

Environment design supports consistent action by making productive behaviours easier.

The Identity Wheel

REFLECTION QUESTIONS

1. In which areas of your life is the knowing-doing gap most evident? What patterns do you notice in situations where you struggle to take action?
2. How has overthinking or perfectionism prevented you from taking important actions in your life?
3. What does "disciplined action" mean to you? When have you experienced the benefits of doing what needs to be done despite not feeling like it?

PRACTICAL EXERCISES

1. Action Archaeology

- Identify three situations:
    - Where you knew what to do and did it successfully
    - Where you knew what to do but didn't follow through
    - Where you took action despite uncertainty
- For each situation, analyse:
    - What thoughts and emotions preceded the action or inaction?
    - What environment or context factors influenced your behaviour?
    - What identity beliefs were at play?

2. Minimal Viable Action

- Choose one goal you've been postponing
- Break it down into the smallest possible first step

- Make this step so minimal that it would feel ridiculous not to do it
- Schedule exactly when you will take this step in the next 24 hours
- After completing it, immediately identify and schedule the next minimal step

3. Three-Day Power List Challenge

- For three consecutive days:
    - Each morning, identify five high-impact actions that would make the day a success
    - Make these actions specific and measurable
    - Commit to completing all five before the day ends
    - At day's end, note which you completed and how it felt
- After three days, reflect on what made completion easier or harder

The Identity Wheel

Chapter 8: Breaking the Confirmation Loop

In the previous chapters, we've explored how the Identity Wheel shows the cyclical nature of our identity, thoughts, emotions, actions and results. We've examined the architecture of the mind that powers this wheel, delved into our core identity statements, explored the power of our thoughts and beliefs, learned how to master our emotional landscape and discovered how to bridge the knowing-doing gap through consistent action. Now, we turn our attention to perhaps the most crucial insight the Identity Wheel offers: understanding and breaking the confirmation loop.

The Self-Fulfilling Nature of the Wheel

Perhaps the most profound insight the Identity Wheel offers is understanding how our results confirm our initial identity. When we act (or don't act) based on our emotions, we create results that often validate our original "I am" statements. This creates a self-fulfilling prophecy, a confirmation loop that can either limit or liberate us, depending on whether we're aware of it and how we choose to engage with it.

The insidious power of confirmation loops becomes most apparent when we trace their operation through someone's actual experience. Kwame's story reveals exactly how these cycles perpetuate themselves.

Kwame adjusted his tie for the fifth time in the elevator, his heart pounding as the floors counted up to the interview that could change his life. Senior Marketing Manager at the company he'd admired for years, but instead of excitement, he felt the familiar dread settling in his chest.

"I always mess up the important opportunities," he muttered, the belief as ingrained as his own name. This wasn't dramatic self-doubt; it was a pattern carved deep by experience. University presentations where his mind went blank. Job interviews where his tongue seemed to forget how to form coherent sentences. Networking events where he'd stumble over introductions and leave feeling humiliated.

The cycle was brutally predictable: big opportunity arose, anxiety flooded his system, poor preparation followed (why invest effort in inevitable failure?), then a hesitant, scattered performance that generated exactly the rejection he'd anticipated. "See?" his internal critic would smugly observe. "I told you so."

This interview followed the script perfectly. Despite having the exact qualifications they wanted, Kwame's answers came out jumbled and defensive. When they asked about his greatest

Chapter 8: Breaking the Confirmation Loop

achievement, he downplayed a campaign that had increased client retention by 40%. When they enquired about leadership experience, he focused on what he hadn't done rather than what he had accomplished.

The rejection email arrived three days later, professionally polite but definitive. Kwame stared at his laptop screen, that familiar cocktail of shame and resignation washing over him. But something was different this time. Instead of accepting defeat, he found himself asking a dangerous question: "What if I'm creating this outcome?"

The thought was simultaneously terrifying and liberating. What if his "unlucky streak" wasn't luck at all but a self-fulfilling prophecy? What if he'd been unconsciously gathering evidence to support a story that wasn't even true?

Kwame decided to test a radical hypothesis: instead of "I always mess up opportunities", what if he chose "I learn from every experience and improve"? The identity shift felt artificial at first, but it generated different thoughts when the next opportunity arose. Instead of catastrophising, he felt curious about what he might discover. That curiosity led to thorough preparation and the confident presentation of his accomplishments.

When the job offer came through (from an even better company) Kwame realised he hadn't gotten luckier. He'd simply stopped sabotaging himself with a story that was never true in the first place.

Kwame's transformation wasn't about becoming more competent; his skills were always sufficient. It was about breaking the confirmation loop that had been creating evidence for a story that was never true in the first place. This is the profound power of recognising self-fulfilling prophecies: once you see them, you can consciously redirect them.

What makes this confirmation loop so powerful is that it operates largely beneath our conscious awareness. We don't typically recognise that we're actively participating in creating evidence that confirms our existing beliefs. Instead, we experience our results as objective reality happening to us rather than a reflection of the self we've programmed ourselves to be.

Recognising Self-Fulfilling Prophecies

The first step in breaking any confirmation loop is recognising that it exists. A self-fulfilling prophecy is a prediction that directly or indirectly causes itself to become true due to positive feedback between belief and behaviour. Once you understand this concept, you'll begin to see these prophecies operating everywhere: In your career, relationships, health, finances and virtually every domain of your life [49].

The primary indicators that you're caught in a self-fulfilling prophecy include:

1. **Recurring Patterns**: You notice the same situations happening repeatedly in your life, almost as if on cue. The characters might change, but the story remains eerily similar [50].
2. **Statements of Resignation**: You catch yourself saying things like "This always happens to me" or "I knew this would happen" when faced with negative outcomes.

Chapter 8: Breaking the Confirmation Loop

3. **Limited Range of Experience**: Your life experiences stay within a predictable range, rarely breaking new ground, even when you consciously desire change.
4. **Emotional Deja Vu**: You experience the same emotional responses to situations, as if following a script that feels both familiar and frustrating.
5. **Confirmation Bias**: You tend to notice and give weight to evidence that supports your existing beliefs while discounting contrary evidence [51].

The Ultimate Confirmation Loop: A Personal Case Study

Let me show you how a confirmation loop can consume years of someone's life without them even recognising it's happening.

At 22, after failing to make it as a professional footballer in America, I carried an identity statement I didn't even realise existed: "I will never amount to anything." This wasn't conscious self-talk, it was my Year 11 history teacher's words, buried so deep in my subconscious that they had become my operating system.

This identity generated predictable thoughts: "Why bother trying?" "Success is for other people." "I always mess things up." These thoughts created emotions of resignation, hopelessness, and a kind of numb despair that felt safer than hope.

These emotions drove equally predictable actions: I drank heavily to numb the pain. I made impulsive business decisions without proper planning. I avoided opportunities that might expose me to failure. I isolated myself from people who believed in me because their faith felt like pressure I couldn't handle.

The results were exactly what my subconscious identity expected: I gained over three stone. My business collapsed. I accumulated thousands of pounds in debt. I ended up back in my childhood bedroom at 28, staring at the same ceiling I'd stared at as a teenager, except now with the "evidence" that I really was worthless.

The confirmation loop was perfect. Every failure proved my history teacher right. Every self-destructive choice generated more evidence that I would "never amount to anything." The wheel kept turning, each rotation making the groove deeper.

What made this loop so insidious was that it felt like objective reality. I wasn't consciously choosing to sabotage myself, I was simply responding logically to who I believed myself to be. Of course someone worthless would make poor decisions. Of course someone destined to fail would avoid taking risks. The actions weren't self-sabotage; they were self-protection.

It took years to recognise that my reality wasn't reflecting some fundamental truth about my who I really was, it was reflecting the mechanical operation of a confirmation loop that had been running since I was sixteen years old.

The moment I saw the pattern, something clicked within me. Not immediately, not easily, but inevitably. Because once you understand that your results are confirming your identity rather than revealing your limitations, you gain access to the most powerful intervention point in the entire system.

Chapter 8: Breaking the Confirmation Loop

The Role of Vibrational Energy in the Confirmation Loop

Many spiritual traditions have long taught what modern quantum physics now confirms – that everything in the universe, including our thoughts and feelings, exists as vibrating energy. As Ralph Waldo Emerson wisely observed, "What you are comes to you." This profound insight gets to the heart of how the confirmation loop operates at an energetic level.

The confirmation loop isn't merely psychological; it's also vibrational. Your identity (those core "I am" statements) determines the energetic frequency at which you vibrate, and this frequency attracts matching experiences, people, opportunities and circumstances. This is why simply changing your conscious thoughts or temporarily shifting your emotional state often fails to create lasting change. The deeper vibrational signature of your identity continues to broadcast and attract corresponding experiences.

When you identify as someone who struggles financially, you vibrate at a frequency that attracts financial challenges. When you identify as someone who enjoys vibrant health, you vibrate at a frequency that attracts health-supporting experiences.

This vibrational resonance explains why so many people struggle to create lasting change despite their best efforts. You might repeat positive affirmations about prosperity while maintaining an underlying identity of scarcity. In such cases, your deeper identity will always win the energetic tug-of-war, pulling your experiences back in alignment with your core "I am" statements.

The Identity Wheel

The universe isn't conspiring against you or for you. It's simply responding to the signal you're broadcasting. If you don't like what you're receiving, change your transmission.

Interrupting Negative Confirmation Loops

Once you recognise that you're caught in a confirmation loop, you gain the power to interrupt it. Like the skilled DJ who can enter the beat at any point, you can step into this cycle and begin creating change wherever you find yourself. Here are specific strategies for interrupting negative loops:

1. Identity Intervention

Since identity sits at the top of the wheel, intervening here creates the most powerful ripple effect throughout the entire system. Begin by questioning your limiting "I am" statements: Are they really true? Where did they come from? What evidence might contradict them?

Create new, empowering identity statements that feel both expansive and believable. Rather than jumping from "I am financially struggling" to "I am a millionaire" (which your subconscious might reject as implausible), try bridge statements like "I am becoming increasingly financially savvy" or "I am developing a prosperity mindset".

Speak these new identity statements aloud daily, preferably while looking in a mirror. This practice might feel uncomfortable at first; that discomfort is simply your subconscious mind resisting the new programming. Persist through this resistance, and the new identity will gradually take root.

2. Thought Pattern Disruption

When you notice thoughts that support your limiting identity, consciously interrupt them. One effective technique is the "cancel-cancel" method: When you catch a negative thought, immediately say "cancel-cancel" (either aloud or mentally) and replace it with a thought aligned with your desired identity.

Another powerful disruption technique is the question method. When a limiting thought arises, question it immediately: "Is this thought serving my growth?" or "Is there another perspective I could take here?" These questions create a pause between the thought and your reaction to it, giving you space to choose a different response.

3. Emotional Pattern Recognition

Emotions serve as valuable feedback about your thought patterns. When you notice an uncomfortable emotion arising, rather than reacting to it or suppressing it, use it as information. Ask yourself: "What thought generated this feeling?" and "What identity statement underlies this thought?"

This awareness allows you to trace the emotion back to its source in your identity structure. From this awareness, you can choose to experience the emotion without being controlled by it and then consciously shift towards emotions aligned with your desired identity.

4. Action Pattern Reversal

Perhaps the most immediately accessible intervention point is your actions. Even when your identity, thoughts and emotions are still aligned with old patterns, you can choose to take actions consistent with your desired identity instead.

This "act as if" approach creates new results that begin challenging your old identity. By consistently taking actions aligned with who you want to become, even when they feel unnatural or uncomfortable, you create evidence that contradicts your limiting beliefs.

Thomas, who identified as "not athletic", committed to taking one small fitness-oriented action each day, regardless of how he felt about it. Some days this was as simple as a five-minute walk; other days it might be a full workout. The consistency of these actions, not their scale, began generating results that challenged his non-athletic identity. Within months, his self-image had shifted to "I am becoming fit", and his actions naturally expanded to match this evolving identity.

5. Results Reinterpretation

The final intervention point is how you interpret the results you create. Most of us automatically interpret our results through the filter of our existing identity, seeing only what confirms our current beliefs.

Practise consciously reinterpreting your results from the perspective of your desired identity. When you experience success, rather than dismissing it as luck or an anomaly, claim it as evidence of your emerging new identity. When you face setbacks, rather than seeing them as confirmation of your limitations, view them as valuable feedback and learning opportunities on your growth journey.

Chapter 8: Breaking the Confirmation Loop

Alexa, who was working to shift her identity from "disorganised" to "systematically organised", noticed that she interpreted her organisational successes as "flukes" while seeing her organisational failures as "proof" of her disorganised nature. By consciously reframing her successes as evidence of her growing organisational skills and her failures as normal learning experiences rather than identity confirmations, she gradually shifted the confirmation loop in a positive direction.

Creating Positive Spirals of Growth

Breaking negative confirmation loops is only half the equation. The other half is intentionally creating positive spirals that reinforce empowering identities. Here are strategies for establishing upward spirals of growth:

1. Evidence Journaling

Start a daily practice of recording evidence that supports your desired identity. Each evening, write down at least three pieces of evidence from that day that confirm your new "I am" statements. These don't need to be dramatic events, even small actions or moments count.

For example, if you're cultivating an identity as "someone who prioritises health" your evidence might include choosing water instead of a soft drink, taking the stairs rather than the lift or going to bed at a reasonable hour. Over time, this growing evidence file becomes a powerful counterweight to your old limiting beliefs.

2. Environmental Engineering

Your physical and social environments powerfully influence your identity confirmation loops. Intentionally engineer environments that support your desired identity rather than triggering old patterns.

This might mean reorganising your physical space to make empowering actions easier, surrounding yourself with people who embody or support your desired identity or changing the media you consume to align with who you're becoming.

3. The Power of Visualisation and Self-Suggestion

The techniques of visualisation and self-suggestion directly address your subconscious programming, helping to install new patterns that support your desired identity.

Spend time each day visualising yourself embodying your new identity, not just seeing it but feeling it as already true. Engage all your senses to make the visualisation as vivid as possible. Deliberate visualisation reprogrammes your subconscious, taking you far beyond daydreaming.

Combine visualisation with self-suggestion by speaking affirmations that support your new identity. The most powerful time for these practices is just before sleep and immediately upon waking, when your subconscious mind is most receptive to new programming.

Chapter 8: Breaking the Confirmation Loop

4. Celebration and Reinforcement

We often focus so intently on our next goal that we fail to celebrate our progress and victories, missing a crucial opportunity to reinforce positive confirmation loops.

Create a regular practice of acknowledging and celebrating evidence of your new identity in action. This celebration doesn't need to be elaborate, simply pausing to feel genuine appreciation and pride in your progress sends a powerful message to your subconscious that this new identity is valuable and worth strengthening.

5. Conscious Identity Expansion

As you successfully replace limiting identities with more empowering ones, don't stop there. The journey of personal growth involves continually expanding your identity to encompass more of your true potential.

Periodically review your core "I am" statements and ask: "What's the next expansion of this identity that would serve my growth?" For instance, once you've established an identity as "financially stable", you might expand to "financially abundant" and later to "financial mentor and leader".

This conscious evolution prevents you from stagnating at any level of achievement and keeps the positive confirmation spiral moving upward.

The Role of Challenges in Breaking Loops

It's important to recognise that challenges and setbacks are not failures of your confirmation loop intervention but essential components of it. When you're working to break established patterns, your subconscious mind will often create resistance in the form of challenges, seeking to pull you back to the familiar territory of your old identity.

Think of these challenges as your opportunity to show your commitment to your new identity. Each time you respond to a challenge from the perspective of who you're becoming rather than who you've been, you strengthen the new pattern and weaken the old one.

Lisa had established a strong identity as a "people pleaser" who avoided conflict at all costs. As she worked to shift to an identity of "confident self-advocate", she found herself facing an unusually high number of situations that required her to set boundaries and speak up for her needs. Rather than seeing these as obstacles, she recognised them as perfect opportunities to practise embodying her new identity. Each time she successfully navigated these situations, even imperfectly, she strengthened her new self-image.

As Abigail N. Rosewood beautifully expressed, "The way we tell stories about ourselves becomes how we view our lives." The universe will always test your new identity to see if you're serious about embodying it. These tests aren't punishments; they're opportunities to prove to yourself that your transformation is real and lasting. Welcome them as confirmation that you're on the right path of growth.

Chapter 8: Breaking the Confirmation Loop

The Energetic Frequency of Growth

As we've explored throughout this chapter, the confirmation loop operates not just psychologically but energetically. When you consistently align your identity, thoughts, emotions and actions with growth rather than limitation, you shift your entire energetic frequency. This shift doesn't just affect your internal experience; it transforms how you interact with the world and what you attract into your life.

People operating at a growth frequency naturally attract opportunities, resources, mentors and circumstances that support their evolution. This reflects how energy naturally interacts. When you vibrate at the frequency of growth, you become sensitive to growth opportunities that were always present but previously invisible to you because you weren't tuned to their frequency.

Think of it like tuning a radio. The stations are always broadcasting, but you can only hear the one to which your receiver is tuned. By consciously tuning your personal frequency to growth, you begin receiving the "broadcasts" that match that frequency: ideas, people, opportunities and resources aligned with expansion rather than contraction.

Tracking Your Progress on the Path

How do you know if you're successfully breaking old confirmation loops and creating positive spirals? Here are key indicators to track:

1. **Expanded Range of Experience**: You find yourself in situations and opportunities that would have been outside your previous identity's scope.
2. **Increased Emotional Flexibility**: You respond to challenges with greater emotional range and resilience rather than falling into habitual emotional patterns.
3. **Surprising Actions**: You sometimes surprise yourself by taking actions that your old identity would have found impossible or unthinkable.
4. **Changed Perception**: You notice details, opportunities and possibilities that were previously invisible to you.
5. **Different Results**: Most tellingly, you begin creating tangibly different results in the areas where you've been working to shift your confirmation loops.

Keep a growth journal to track these indicators over time. Human beings are notorious for forgetting how far they've come, so documenting your journey provides concrete evidence of your evolution that you can revisit whenever you need encouragement.

The Promise of Breaking the Confirmation Loop

As we conclude this exploration of the confirmation loop within the Identity Wheel framework, let's consider what becomes possible when you master this aspect of personal transformation. Breaking negative confirmation loops and creating positive spirals of growth isn't just about improving specific areas of your life, though it certainly does that. More profoundly, it's about freeing yourself from unconscious programming and claiming the power to consciously create your experience.

Chapter 8: Breaking the Confirmation Loop

When you understand how the confirmation loop operates and develop the skills to intervene effectively, you gain freedom from repeating the same limiting patterns throughout your life. You're no longer destined to recreate the same struggles in different settings; instead, you become the conscious author of your life story.

Moreover, you develop the capacity for continuous evolution. Rather than reaching a plateau of growth and remaining there, you establish an ongoing spiral of expansion that can continue throughout your lifetime. Each new level of achievement becomes the foundation for the next evolution, creating a life of perpetual growth and discovery.

Perhaps most significantly, breaking the confirmation loop allows you to align more fully with your authentic self, the person you were designed to be before limiting beliefs and identities took hold. As you shed the constraints of outdated programming, you uncover more of your natural gifts, passions and purpose.

Looking Ahead

Every result you receive is part of a larger conversation, with yourself, your identity and the universe. It's not just feedback – it's direction.

The patterns that repeat in your life aren't accidents. They're confirmation loops, echoes of your current beliefs. But when seen clearly, they become portals.

In the next chapter, we'll explore how your mindset acts as the operating system of your entire reality. You'll learn how attitude,

The Identity Wheel

gratitude and emotional resilience act as stabilisers that keep the wheel turning in the direction of your growth, even in moments of resistance or difficulty.

For now, reflect on the loops that keep circling back in your own life. What identity are they confirming? What might happen if you interrupted just one of them with a new thought, a braver action or a more compassionate self-perception?

The Identity Wheel is always in motion.

But now, with awareness in your hands and tools at your side, you are no longer a passive passenger.

The loop that once trapped you is now your lever for transformation.

Chapter 8: Breaking the Confirmation Loop

Chapter Summary

Results confirm initial identity in a self-fulfilling prophecy that strengthens with repetition.

Self-fulfilling prophecies show up as recurring patterns, statements of resignation, limited experiences, emotional déjà vu and confirmation bias.

Vibrational energy of identity attracts matching experiences, explaining why surface-level changes often fail.

Negative loops can be interrupted at any point: identity intervention, thought pattern disruption, emotional pattern recognition, action pattern reversal or results reinterpretation.

Positive spirals can be created through evidence journaling, environmental engineering, visualisation and self-suggestion, celebration and reinforcement and conscious identity expansion.

Challenges are essential for breaking established patterns, providing opportunities to show commitment to new identity.

Energy alignment shifts your frequency, making you receptive to previously invisible opportunities.

Progress indicators include expanded experience range, emotional flexibility, surprising actions, changed perception and different results.

The Identity Wheel

REFLECTION QUESTIONS

1. What self-fulfilling prophecies do you recognise in your life? How have your expectations created the very experiences that confirm them?
2. Which areas of your life show the strongest confirmation loops, where results consistently reinforce your initial beliefs?
3. How might consciously interrupting these loops change your life experience?

PRACTICAL EXERCISES

1. Loop Detection

- Identify three recurring patterns in your life
- For each pattern, trace the full confirmation loop:
    - Identity: What do you believe about yourself?
    - Thoughts: What thoughts does this belief generate?
    - Emotions: What feelings arise from these thoughts?
    - Actions: What behaviours result from these feelings?
    - Results: What outcomes do these actions create?
    - Confirmation: How do these results reinforce your original belief?
- Circle one loop you'd most like to transform

2. Pattern Interruption Planning

- For the loop you circled above:

Chapter 8: Breaking the Confirmation Loop

- o Identity: What alternative belief could you consider?
- o Thoughts: What different thoughts would arise from this new belief?
- o Emotions: What feelings would these new thoughts generate?
- o Actions: What behaviours would naturally follow?
- o Results: What different outcomes might these actions create?
- Identify the easiest point for you to interrupt this loop (identity, thoughts, emotions or actions)

3. Evidence Journal Start-up

- Choose one limiting belief you want to challenge
- Create a small notebook or digital note dedicated to collecting evidence that contradicts this belief
- Set a goal to find and record at least one piece of contradictory evidence daily for one week
- Notice how actively looking for this evidence changes what you perceive

The Identity Wheel

Chapter 9: Transforming Your Reality Through Mindset

In the previous chapters, we've explored the Identity Wheel's cyclical nature, understood the architecture of mind, delved into our core identity, examined the power of thoughts and beliefs, learned to master our emotional landscape, discovered how to bridge the knowing-doing gap and worked on breaking negative confirmation loops. Now, we're ready to explore how mindset fundamentally shapes our reality and transforms our life experience.

Your mindset isn't something you have; it's something you practise. Every thought you think is either strengthening the mindset that serves you or the one that limits you.

The Power of Attitude in Shaping Reality

Your attitude is like a lens through which you perceive and interact with the world. Think of it as a comprehensive filter- beyond fleeting moods - that determines what you notice, how you interpret experiences, and how you respond to life's challenges and opportunities.

William James of Harvard University, often called the father of psychology in America, said: "Human beings can alter their lives by altering their attitudes of mind." This statement isn't philosophical rhetoric; it's a practical truth demonstrated repeatedly through both scientific research and lived experience [52].

Consider Sarah and James, colleagues who both face the same company-wide restructuring. Sarah, with her solution-oriented attitude, immediately begins identifying potential opportunities in the change: new roles she might qualify for, skills she could develop or ways her department might benefit. James, however, with his threat-focused attitude, sees only potential dangers: job loss, increased workload or unfavourable changes to company culture.

Though they occupy the same physical workspace and receive the same information, Sarah and James are experiencing entirely different realities. Sarah's attitude opens pathways to growth and advancement, while James's attitude creates stress and limitation. The restructuring itself is neutral; it's their attitudes that shape their experiences and ultimately their outcomes.

Chapter 9: Transforming Your Reality Through Mindset

Becoming Intentional About Your Mental State

The power of attitude reveals that transforming your reality begins with becoming intentional about your mental state. Most people allow their mental state to be determined reactively by external circumstances, shifting with every challenge or disappointment like a sailboat without a rudder.

Becoming intentional means taking the helm of your mental state rather than allowing it to be buffeted by external forces. It means recognising that most of your mental state is a choice, not a condition imposed upon you by circumstances.

This intentionality requires developing what psychologists call "metacognition" (the awareness of your own thinking). When you cultivate metacognition, you create a space between stimulus and response, allowing you to choose your mental state rather than merely reacting.

For example, when faced with a setback, most people automatically cascade into frustration, disappointment or even despair. Their thought patterns follow well-worn neural pathways of negativity, often established in childhood. The intentional person, however, pauses after the setback, acknowledges the initial emotional response, and then consciously chooses a more empowering mental state.

To become intentional about your mental state, you must first become aware of your current patterns. The following exercise can help you develop this awareness:

For one week, set a reminder on your phone to check in with your mental state every two hours during waking hours. When the reminder sounds, pause and ask yourself:

1. What is my current mental state?
2. What triggered this state?
3. Is this mental state serving my goals and well-being?
4. If not, what mental state would better serve me?

This simple exercise builds the metacognitive muscles that allow you to become more intentional about your mental state. Over time, you'll develop the ability to notice your mental state without the reminder and, more importantly, to shift it intentionally when needed.

The Mental Contrasting Technique

One powerful method for transforming your mindset is a practice called mental contrasting, developed by psychologist Gabriele Oettingen. This technique helps bridge the gap between positive thinking and realistic planning in a way that energises rather than depletes you [53].

Mental contrasting works in four steps, forming the acronym WOOP:

1. **Wish**: Identify a meaningful, challenging but feasible wish or goal.
2. **Outcome**: Imagine the best outcome from achieving this wish in vivid detail. Feel the positive emotions associated with this outcome.

3. **Obstacle**: Identify the main internal obstacle that might prevent you from fulfilling your wish.
4. **Plan**: Create an if-then plan to overcome the obstacle: "If [obstacle] occurs, then I will [specific action]."

What makes mental contrasting so effective is that it doesn't rely solely on positive visualisation, which research shows can actually reduce motivation by providing a premature sense of accomplishment. Instead, it harnesses the motivational energy from both the desired future and the recognition of obstacles.

The Mindset Ecology: Your Environment Shapes Your Thinking

We often think of mindset as purely internal, but research increasingly shows that our environment plays a crucial role in shaping how we think. Your mindset exists within an ecology of influences that either support or undermine your desired way of thinking.

Consider these key elements of your mindset ecology:

1. Physical Environment

Your physical surroundings constantly send subtle cues to your brain about what's important, what's possible and how you should behave. Think about it – have you ever noticed how differently you feel and think in a cluttered room versus a tidy one? Or how a space with natural light affects your mood compared to fluorescent lighting?

This isn't just your imagination. Researchers at the University of Minnesota found something fascinating – when people spent time in an orderly room, they made healthier choices and were more generous. But here's the twist: when they sat in a messy room, their creativity actually increased! [54] Neither environment was "better" – they simply brought out different parts of people's thinking.

Have you ever considered how your own spaces might be programming your thoughts without you even realising it?

To consciously shape your mindset through your physical environment:

- Create dedicated spaces that support specific mental states. For example, designate one area for focused work that's free from distractions and another for creative thinking that contains stimulating visuals or objects.
- Introduce visual cues aligned with your aspirational mindset. These might include quotes, images or symbolic objects that remind you of the mindset you're cultivating.
- Modify your lighting. Research shows that brighter lighting intensifies emotions (both positive and negative) and can lead to more analytical thinking, while dimmer lighting can promote relaxation and sometimes more creative thinking.

2. Social Environment

Who do you spend most of your time with? Your answer matters far more than you might think. The people around you shape your mindset through something scientists call "social contagion" – basically, you catch thoughts and feelings from others just like you'd catch a cold! [55]

Chapter 9: Transforming Your Reality Through Mindset

Here's something that might surprise you: when someone close to you becomes happier, your own chances of becoming happier jump by 25% [56]. And it's not just happiness – everything from health habits to work ethic can spread through your social connections.

Think about your five closest relationships for a moment. Are they lifting you towards the mindset you want to develop or are they subtly pulling you away from it? This isn't about judging those relationships – it's about recognising their profound impact on how you think.

To create a social environment that supports your desired mindset:

- Audit your five closest relationships. These people have the most significant impact on your mindset. Do they reinforce the mindset you're trying to cultivate, or do they undermine it?
- Create a "mental model advisory board" of people, living or dead, whose mindsets you admire. Read their work, study their thinking processes, and regularly ask yourself, "How would [person] approach this situation?"
- Actively seek out communities organised around the mindset you wish to cultivate. These might be formal groups like mastermind circles or informal relationships with like-minded people.

3. Informational Environment

What was the first thing you consumed this morning? I'm not talking about breakfast – I'm talking about information. Was it the news? Social media? Emails?

Just as food becomes your body, information becomes your thoughts. And just like junk food, some information diets can leave your mind feeling foggy and negative.

Want proof? In one eye-opening study, people who watched just three minutes of negative news in the morning were 27% more likely to report having a bad day six to eight hours later [57]. Three minutes! That's probably less time than you spend brushing your teeth.

When was the last time you took a hard look at what's feeding your mind each day? What might change if you became as intentional about your information diet as many people are about their food choices?

To optimise your informational environment:

- Conduct an information audit. Track what information you consume over a typical week and evaluate its impact on your mindset.
- Implement strategic information boundaries. These might include time-blocking your news consumption, unsubscribing from sources that consistently trigger negative thought patterns or using technology tools to filter content.

Chapter 9: Transforming Your Reality Through Mindset

- Create an intentional learning curriculum around the mindset you wish to develop. This could include books, courses or discussions specifically chosen to strengthen your desired thinking patterns.

4. Biological Environment

Have you ever noticed you're brilliant at solving problems at certain times of day, but your brain feels like it's wading through treacle at others? That's not random. It's your internal clock at work.

Your brain doesn't maintain the same thinking capacity throughout the day. For most of us, our analytical superpowers peak about 2-4 hours after waking up. Creative thinking, interestingly enough, often flourishes when we're a bit tired.

Think about your own daily rhythms for a moment. When do you feel sharpest? When do your best ideas tend to strike? The mismatch between when you schedule important mental work and when your brain is actually primed for that type of thinking might explain why some tasks feel unnecessarily difficult.

What if you started working with your natural mental rhythms instead of against them?

To optimise your biological environment:

- Align your most important mental work with your peak cognitive periods. For example, schedule strategic thinking when your analytical capacity is highest.
- Create transition rituals between different types of activities. These help your brain shift from one mindset to

another, such as a short walk between focused work and creative thinking.
- Build in regular periods of mental rest and renewal. Research shows that cognitive performance declines without adequate recovery, similar to physical performance.

By consciously designing these four aspects of your mindset ecology, you create an environment that naturally pulls you towards your desired ways of thinking rather than having to rely solely on willpower and conscious effort.

The Mindset Spectrum: Moving Beyond Binary Thinking

Most discussions about mindset focus on dualities: fixed vs. growth mindset, scarcity vs. abundance, pessimistic vs. optimistic. While these distinctions can be useful starting points, they can also trap us in oversimplified binary thinking.

A more nuanced approach recognises that effective mindsets exist on a spectrum and that different situations may call for different mindset positions. Rather than trying to permanently adopt one end of the spectrum, mental flexibility allows you to consciously select the most appropriate mindset for each situation.

Consider these three mindset spectrums:

1. Analysis ↔ Synthesis

The analytical mindset breaks things down into their component parts to understand how they work. The synthetic mindset combines elements to create something new. We need both, but many of us default heavily to one end of this spectrum.

Chapter 9: Transforming Your Reality Through Mindset

Engineers, lawyers and scientists often excel at analysis but may struggle with synthesis. Artists, entrepreneurs and visionaries might excel at synthesis but lack analytical rigour. The most effective thinkers can move fluidly between these modes.

To develop flexibility on this spectrum:

- If you're naturally analytical, practise "possibility thinking" by asking, "What else could this mean?" or "How might these elements combine in unexpected ways?"
- If you're naturally synthetic, strengthen your analytical skills by asking, "What are the component parts here?" or "What evidence supports or contradicts this vision?"

2. Certainty ↔ Curiosity

The certainty mindset seeks closure, clear answers and definitive positions. The curiosity mindset embraces questions, explores multiple perspectives and remains open to new information.

Both have their place. Certainty helps us make decisions and take action; curiosity helps us learn, innovate and adapt. Problems arise when we get stuck at either extreme: either unable to reach conclusions or closed to new evidence.

To develop flexibility on this spectrum:

- If you tend towards excessive certainty, practise asking questions that open possibilities: "What am I missing?" or "What would change my mind about this?"
- If you tend towards endless curiosity without closure, practise decision frameworks that help you reach

conclusions, such as, "Based on what I know now, the best decision appears to be..."

3. Individual ↔ Collective

The individualistic mindset focuses on personal agency, achievements and responsibilities. The collective mindset emphasises interconnection, shared outcomes and system-level thinking.

Western cultures typically skew towards individualism, while many Eastern cultures emphasise collectivism. Both perspectives offer valuable insights, and the most effective mindset incorporates elements of each.

To develop flexibility on this spectrum:

- If you naturally think in individualistic terms, practise systems thinking by asking, "How does this affect the broader community?" or "What collective resources make my individual achievement possible?"
- If you naturally emphasise collective perspectives, strengthen your sense of agency by asking, "What unique contribution can I make here?" or "How can I take personal responsibility within this system?"

By developing fluency across these spectrums, you build a mental repertoire that allows you to adapt your mindset to different situations rather than forcing every circumstance to fit a single mental model.

Chapter 9: Transforming Your Reality Through Mindset

Cognitive Reappraisal: Changing the Meaning of Experiences

One of the most powerful mindset tools revealed by contemporary research is cognitive reappraisal, the deliberate reinterpretation of a situation to change its emotional impact. This technique works because emotions don't stem directly from events but from the meaning we assign to those events.

A groundbreaking study by James Gross at Stanford University showed that participants who used cognitive reappraisal when viewing disturbing images showed decreased negative emotional responses and increased positive emotional responses, compared to those who simply tried to suppress their reactions [58].

What makes cognitive reappraisal particularly valuable is that, unlike suppression, it doesn't require ongoing mental effort. Once you've shifted the meaning of a situation, the emotional change happens naturally.

Here are three effective forms of cognitive reappraisal:

1. Distancing

Distancing involves observing your situation from a different perspective, as if you were watching someone else or viewing yourself from a distance. This creates psychological space that dampens intense emotions and enables more objective thinking.

To practise distancing:

- Use third-person language when thinking about your situation. Instead of "I'm facing a crisis" try "Daniel is

facing a challenge". This simple linguistic shift creates immediate cognitive distance.
- Imagine viewing your situation from a physical distance, such as from a balcony or a hilltop. What details become less prominent? What patterns become more visible?
- Project yourself into the future and look back on the current situation. How might you view this challenge five years from now?

2. Reframing

Reframing involves finding an alternative interpretation of a situation that changes its emotional significance while still acknowledging reality. Unlike positive thinking that may deny difficulties, reframing finds legitimate alternative meanings.

To practise reframing:

- Ask yourself, "What else could this mean?" or "How else might I interpret what's happening?"
- Look for the opportunity within the setback. Not "This is good" (which may be untrue), but rather "This contains something valuable" (which is almost always possible).
- Consider how someone you admire might interpret the same situation differently.

3. Broader Contextualisation

This form of reappraisal places the current situation in a larger context, revealing patterns and meaning that might not be visible when focusing narrowly on immediate circumstances.

To practise broader contextualisation:

- Place the current challenge in the context of your entire life journey. How does it connect to previous challenges you've overcome?
- Consider how this experience might be preparing you for future contributions or achievements. What capabilities might it be developing?
- Reflect on how your experience connects to broader human themes or archetypal journeys. How might your struggle reflect universal aspects of the human condition?

Cognitive reappraisal doesn't eliminate difficulties, but it transforms how we experience them. By changing the meaning we assign to challenging situations, we change how they affect us emotionally, which in turn influences the actions we take and the results we create.

Pragmatic Optimism: The Middle Path

When discussing mindset, we often encounter two problematic extremes. At one end lies toxic positivity, the insistence on positive thinking regardless of circumstances, which can lead to denial and emotional suppression. At the other end lies cynical pessimism, a consistently negative outlook that, while sometimes presenting as "realism", actually distorts reality through its negative bias.

Between these extremes lies a more effective approach: pragmatic optimism. This mindset combines positive expectation with a clear-eyed assessment of reality.

Optimism without action is delusion. Pessimism without action is paralysis. Pragmatic optimism is hope with a plan.

Martin Seligman, founder of positive psychology, discovered through his research that optimists and pessimists differ primarily in how they explain events to themselves. These explanatory styles have three dimensions: [59]

1. **Permanence**: Optimists see negative events as temporary ("This project is challenging") while pessimists see them as permanent ("Projects are always nightmares").
2. **Pervasiveness**: Optimists contain difficulties to specific areas ("I struggled with this presentation") while pessimists globalise them ("I'm terrible at communication").
3. **Personalisation**: When good things happen, optimists see their role in creating success ("My preparation paid off") while pessimists attribute it to external factors or luck ("Anyone could have done it").

The pragmatic optimist adopts the optimistic explanatory style while still acknowledging difficulties. Rather than denying challenges, they frame them as specific, temporary and manageable. This creates the psychological space needed to respond effectively.

This mindset is particularly powerful during periods of change or uncertainty. When facing disruption, the pragmatic optimist asks: "Given this new reality, what opportunities can I create?" Rather than wasting energy resisting what cannot be changed, they direct their focus towards what can be influenced or created.

Chapter 9: Transforming Your Reality Through Mindset

Creating Your Mindset Transformation System

Having explored these concepts, it's time to integrate them into a personal mindset transformation system. This isn't about occasional mindset shifts but instead about creating a comprehensive approach that gradually rewires your default ways of thinking.

A complete mindset transformation system includes these five components:

1. Daily Practices

These are brief, consistent activities that gradually reshape your mental habits over time. Effective daily practices might include:

- A morning mental rehearsal where you visualise navigating the day's challenges with your desired mindset
- A midday mindset check-in that helps you course-correct if you've drifted into unproductive thinking
- An evening reflection that highlights moments when you successfully embodied your target mindset

2. Environmental Design

As we've discussed, your environment powerfully shapes your thinking. Implement at least one modification to each aspect of your environment:

- Physical: Create a space that visually reinforces your desired mindset
- Social: Schedule regular interaction with people who embody the mindset you're developing

- Informational: Curate your inputs to prioritise content that strengthens your target mindset
- Biological: Structure your time to support mental states aligned with your goals

3. Trigger Response Planning

Identify specific situations that typically trigger unproductive mindsets for you and develop pre-planned responses:

- Name three common triggers that activate limiting mindsets for you
- For each trigger, create an if-then implementation intention: "If [trigger occurs], then I will [specific response]"
- Practise these responses mentally until they become automatic

4. Mindset Measurement

What gets measured improves. Create a simple system to track your mindset over time:

- Identify 2–3 observable indicators that your mindset is shifting in the desired direction
- Create a simple scale to rate yourself daily or weekly on these indicators
- Review trends monthly to identify patterns and adjust your approach

5. Recovery Protocols

Even with a strong system, you'll occasionally fall into old thinking patterns. Having pre-established recovery protocols helps you bounce back quickly:

- Create a "mindset reset" ritual you can use when you notice you've slipped into old patterns
- Identify supportive resources you can access during challenging periods
- Establish clear criteria for when to seek additional support from mentors or coaches

By implementing all five components, you create a robust system that not only initiates mindset change but sustains it over time, gradually transforming how you perceive and interact with reality.

The Identity Wheel as a Reality-Creation Process

As we conclude this chapter, let's bring these concepts together by revisiting the Identity Wheel from Chapter 1 and understanding how it functions as a dynamic reality-creation process.

The Identity Wheel illustrates precisely how your mindset shapes your reality. Your identity (the hub of the wheel) influences your thoughts, which generate emotions, which drive actions, which produce results, which then circle back to either confirm or challenge your original identity. This cycle operates continuously, whether you're conscious of it or not.

The transformative insight from our exploration of mindset is that you can intervene at any point in the Identity Wheel to change its direction. You can directly shift your identity and thoughts using the mindset techniques we've explored, modify your environment to support different perceptions, regulate your emotions using cognitive reappraisal, or take new actions that create results that gradually reshape your identity.

The most powerful transformation occurs when you intervene at multiple points of the Identity Wheel simultaneously, creating a positive spiral where each element reinforces the others. As your mindset improves, you notice more opportunities, which generates positive emotions, which energises effective action, which produces encouraging results, which further strengthens your empowering identity.

This virtuous cycle is available to anyone willing to engage thoughtfully with their own mental processes. The Identity Wheel keeps turning, but with the mindset insights and techniques from this chapter, you now have greater influence over its direction.

Chapter 9: Transforming Your Reality Through Mindset

Looking Ahead

Having explored how to transform your reality through mindset, we're now prepared to address the crucial question of sustainability: How do you maintain these changes over the long term? In the next chapter, we'll discover the key to maintaining discipline, explore the mountain/valley visualisation of transformation journeys and learn how to protect your transformation from negative influences. We'll also delve into the process of reviewing, reflecting on and rewiring your mindset to ensure continued growth beyond the initial transformation.

For now, begin implementing your mindset transformation system by selecting one daily practice, one environmental modification and one trigger response plan to implement this week. Remember that mindset transformation isn't an event but a process, one that unfolds through consistent, conscious engagement with your own mental ecology.

Chapter Summary

Attitude functions as a lens determining what you notice, how you interpret experiences and how you respond.

Intentional mental states require metacognition (awareness of your own thinking).

Mental contrasting bridges positive thinking and realistic planning through the WOOP technique (Wish, Outcome, Obstacle, Plan).

Mindset ecology comprises physical, social, informational and biological environments that shape thinking.

The mindset spectrum moves beyond binary thinking to develop flexibility across analysis/synthesis, certainty/curiosity and individual/collective dimensions.

Cognitive reappraisal changes emotional impact through distancing, reframing and broader contextualisation.

Pragmatic optimism combines positive expectation with a clear-eyed assessment of reality.

A complete mindset transformation system includes daily practices, environmental design, trigger response planning, mindset measurement and recovery protocols.

Chapter 9: Transforming Your Reality Through Mindset

REFLECTION QUESTIONS

1. How would you describe your current dominant mindset? How has this mindset shaped what you notice and experience?
2. Which aspects of your mindset ecology (physical, social, informational, biological) most strongly influence your thinking patterns?
3. What might change if you approached challenges with pragmatic optimism rather than either toxic positivity or cynical pessimism?

PRACTICAL EXERCISES

1. Mindset Awareness Check

- For two days, set a timer to check your mindset every 3 hours while awake
- Each time, note:
    - What is my current mental state?
    - What triggered this state?
    - Is this mindset serving me in this moment?
    - What mindset would better serve my goals right now?
- After two days, identify your most common unproductive mindsets and their triggers

2. Mindset Ecology Audit

- Assess each dimension of your mindset ecology:
    - Physical: How does your physical environment support or undermine your desired mindset?

The Identity Wheel

- Social: Which relationships elevate your thinking and which limit it?
- Informational: What content do you consume regularly and how does it affect you?
- Temporal: When during the day is your mind most receptive to positive input?
- Identify one modification to make in each dimension

3. Cognitive Reappraisal Practice

- Select a current challenge you're facing
- Practise all three forms of cognitive reappraisal:
    - Distancing: View the situation as if it were happening to a friend
    - Reframing: Identify three alternative interpretations of what's happening
    - Broader Contextualisation: Consider how this fits into your larger life journey
- Note which approach feels most helpful for this particular situation

Chapter 10: Sustaining Your Transformation

You've come so far on this journey.

Take a moment to reflect on where you were when you first opened this book compared to where you are now. The awareness you've developed, the mental programmes you've questioned, the boundaries you've established – these aren't small achievements. They represent fundamental shifts in how you relate to yourself and the world around you.

But transformation isn't a destination; it's an ongoing process.

The question now becomes: how do you sustain this growth? How do you prevent yourself from sliding back into old patterns when life inevitably throws challenges your way?

This chapter is about embedding your transformation so deeply that it becomes your new normal. It's about creating systems that support you even when motivation wanes and developing practices that continuously reinforce your evolution.

The Framework for Lasting Change

Throughout this book, we've explored the Identity Wheel: how your thoughts lead to your feelings, which drive your actions, which create your results, which reinforce your identity. This cycle is key to understanding not just how change happens but how to make it stick.

Lasting change requires alignment across all levels of this wheel. You can't just change your actions and expect transformation to stick. You need to address the entire system.

For change to truly last, you need alignment across five key elements:

1. **Identity shift:** See yourself as already being your 2.0 version
2. **Thought patterns:** Cultivate thinking that supports your new identity
3. **Emotional alignment:** Connect emotionally to your transformation
4. **Consistent actions:** Take steps that express your authentic self
5. **Environmental support:** Design your surroundings to reinforce change

When these elements work together, change doesn't require constant struggle, it flows naturally from who you've become.

Let's now explore powerful practices that will help you maintain this alignment and sustain your transformation long term.

The Challenge of Maintaining Change: Energy vs. Entropy

Research suggests that only 5-20% of people maintain their positive changes long term [60]. The odds might seem stacked against you, but I want you to be in that percentage who succeed.

To understand why sustainability is so challenging, we need to appreciate a fundamental principle that governs not just human behaviour but the entire universe: the relationship between energy and entropy.

Understanding Entropy in Your Life

The Second Law of Thermodynamics states that entropy (the measure of disorder in a system) naturally increases over time unless energy is deliberately applied to maintain order. This physical law governs every aspect of our lives: everything naturally tends to fall apart, become disorganised, or deteriorate unless we actively put effort into maintaining it.

Nobel Prize-winning chemist Ilya Prigogine described humans as "dissipative structures": systems that can temporarily reverse entropy by consuming energy. Unlike inanimate objects that inevitably break down, we can actually grow, develop and become more organised but only through the consistent application of energy [61].

Consider these examples of entropy at work in everyday life:

- A clean room doesn't stay clean without regular tidying
- A fit body doesn't remain fit without continued exercise
- A sharp mind doesn't stay sharp without intellectual stimulation
- A business doesn't maintain success without ongoing innovation
- A language isn't retained without practice

Each of these represents a system that naturally moves towards disorder unless energy is consistently applied.

The Energy Cost of Transformation

Your personal transformation is no different. The new neural pathways, habits, boundaries and paradigm shifts you've developed throughout this book all require energy to maintain. Without this energy, the natural pull of entropy will gradually return you to your previous state, often without you even noticing it's happening.

This explains why so many people start strong with positive changes but gradually slide back into old patterns. They underestimate the energy required to overcome the natural pull of entropy.

Psychologist Dr Kelly McGonigal refers to this as "willpower depletion", the idea that self-control is a limited resource that gets consumed as you use it. While more recent research suggests willpower may not be quite as finite as once thought, there's no question that maintaining change requires consistent energy expenditure [62].

Neurologically, this makes perfect sense. Your old patterns represent well-established neural pathways, which are like superhighways in your brain that require minimal energy to travel. Your new patterns are more like footpaths through dense forest, requiring significantly more energy to traverse. Initially, at least.

Energy Sources for Sustainable Change

Energy is powerful enough to overcome entropy, but only when applied consistently.

The good news is that you can draw on multiple sources of energy to maintain your transformation:

1. **Physical energy:** Proper nutrition, sleep and exercise create the foundation for all other forms of energy. Research by Dr Jim Loehr at the Human Performance Institute shows that physical energy management is the cornerstone of sustainable high performance [63].
2. **Emotional energy:** Positive emotions like inspiration, gratitude and purpose generate sustainable energy. Psychologist Barbara Fredrickson's "broaden-and-build" theory shows how positive emotions expand our resources and increase resilience [64].
3. **Mental energy:** Focus and mindfulness conserve energy by eliminating wasteful thinking. Neuroscientist Dr Amishi Jha's research shows how mindfulness practices improve attention allocation and cognitive efficiency [65].

4. **Spiritual energy:** Connection to something larger than yourself, whether through religious practice, nature, art or community, provides renewable energy that transcends personal limitations.
5. **Social energy:** Supportive relationships amplify your available energy. Research by social psychologist Dr Heidi Grant shows that the right kind of social support actually reduces the perceived energy cost of difficult tasks. [66]

Think of your transformation like tending a garden. A garden left untended doesn't remain beautiful – it becomes overgrown with weeds. A relationship without attention doesn't stay vibrant – it withers. Your transformation works the same way. Without continued energy directed towards your growth, old patterns (the weeds) will reassert themselves.

This isn't meant to discourage you. It's meant to prepare you. By understanding this fundamental truth, you can develop strategies to counteract entropy, not through unsustainable bursts of willpower, but through intelligent energy management and the systems we'll explore in the rest of this chapter.

Winning the Day: A Brief Reminder

We've already explored the Power List concept in previous chapters, so I'll just offer a quick reminder: focus on winning the next 24 hours rather than becoming overwhelmed by long-term goals. Complete your five key actions and you've won the day regardless of what else happens.

Remember, if you win just four days out of seven, you've won the week. Never have two bad days in a row. This simple practice creates consistency that compounds over time.

The Transformative Science of Meditation

Few practices have been as instrumental in my personal transformation as meditation. The tattoo of a meditating man composed of the universe on my right arm isn't just body art, it's a permanent reminder of the practice that helped free me from the mental prison I once lived in.

Beyond Relaxation: The Neuroscience of Meditation

While many view meditation simply as a relaxation technique, the science reveals something far more profound: meditation literally rewires your brain.

Dr Sara Lazar, a neuroscientist at Harvard Medical School, conducted groundbreaking research using MRI scans to examine the brains of long-term meditators. Her team discovered that meditation doesn't just create temporary states of calm; it creates enduring changes in brain structure and function [67].

Her research revealed something remarkable: meditation doesn't just create temporary states of calm; it creates enduring changes in both brain structure and function. The changes weren't limited to individual brain regions but extended to how these regions communicated with one another.

Specifically, her research showed:

- Increased grey matter in the prefrontal cortex, associated with higher-order brain functions like awareness, concentration and decision-making
- Reduced grey matter in the amygdala, the brain's "fight or flight" centre associated with fear, anxiety and stress
- Preserved grey matter in the brain with age (non-meditators showed typical age-related decline in grey matter, while meditators in their 50s had the same amount of grey matter as those in their 20s)

Focused attention fundamentally restructures the brain's architecture.

The goal of meditation, is to transform your relationship with thoughts, not eliminate them.

Brain Waves: Shifting Gears in Consciousness

Your brain operates at different electrical frequencies throughout the day, measured as brain waves:

- **Beta waves (14–30 Hz)**: Your normal waking state: analytical, sometimes stressed
- **Alpha waves (8–13.9 Hz)**: Relaxed awareness: creative, learning-oriented
- **Theta waves (4–7.9 Hz)**: Deep meditation or light sleep: intuitive, imaginative
- **Delta waves (0.5–3.9 Hz)**: Deep, dreamless sleep: healing, regenerative
- **Gamma waves (30–100 Hz)**: Higher consciousness: integration, compassion

Chapter 10: Sustaining Your Transformation

Dr Richard Davidson's research at the Centre for Healthy Minds discovered that experienced meditators could intentionally shift between these states, accessing theta and gamma waves during deep meditation whilst remaining fully conscious [68]. His findings demonstrated that meditation allows people to develop unprecedented control over their mental experience, moving fluidly between different states of consciousness. The implications were profound: we can intentionally change our brains and improve our health and wellbeing through practice alone.

Most of us remain stuck in a beta state: analytical, sometimes anxious, and often exhausting. Meditation trains your brain to access alpha and theta states at will, creating a more balanced internal experience.

The Default Mode Network: Quieting the Monkey Mind

Perhaps one of the most significant discoveries in meditation research involves what neuroscientists call the Default Mode Network (DMN) – the brain regions active when you're not focused on the outside world, often referred to as the "monkey mind".

Dr Judson Brewer's research at Brown University's Mindfulness Centre showed that the DMN acts as our brain's autopilot, constantly engaged in rumination about the past and worry about the future. This network reinforces our sense of separate self and strengthens the stories we tell about ourselves. [69]

His research demonstrated that meditation quiets this network, allowing meditators to step out of rumination and self-referential thinking.

This explains why meditation creates a sense of spaciousness and perspective, you're literally deactivating the brain network responsible for self-centred thinking.

As Buddhist monk Matthieu Ricard, who has been called "the happiest man in the world" based on brain scans of his positive emotions during meditation, puts it: "Meditation is not just blissing out under a mango tree. It completely changes your brain and therefore changes what you are."

Practical Applications: Beyond the Cushion

These neurological changes translate into practical benefits that extend far beyond your meditation sessions:

1. **Enhanced emotional regulation:** Research by Dr Philippe Goldin found that just eight weeks of meditation training increased activation in the prefrontal regions that manage emotional responses while decreasing activation in the amygdala. This means you respond rather than react to emotional triggers.
2. **Improved focus and cognition:** A study published in the journal *Psychological Science* found that meditation training improved participants' ability to sustain attention and process information quickly and accurately, even during boring, repetitive tasks.
3. **Reduced stress and anxiety:** Multiple studies have shown that meditation reduces cortisol (the stress hormone) levels and increases activity in brain regions associated with positive emotions.
4. **Physical health benefits:** Research published in the *Journal of Alternative and Complementary Medicine* found

that meditation practices lower blood pressure, strengthen immune function and reduce inflammation markers.
5. **Enhanced self-awareness:** A study in the journal *Frontiers in Human Neuroscience* found that meditation increases activation in brain areas associated with introspection and metacognition (your ability to observe your own thoughts and feelings objectively).

As neuroscientist Dr Richard Davidson summarises: "What we're finding about meditation would be front-page news if it were a drug. The fact that we can intentionally change our brains and improve our health and well-being is revolutionary."

Getting Started: Simple Yet Profound

You don't need special equipment, years of practice or spiritual beliefs to benefit from meditation. You just need to begin.

Start with five minutes daily, gradually building to 20 minutes or more. Find a quiet space, sit comfortably with your back supported, and try this simple practice:

1. **Focus on your breath.** Notice the sensation of air entering and leaving your nostrils or the rise and fall of your chest.
2. **When your mind wanders (and it will), gently bring your attention back to your breath.** Don't judge yourself for getting distracted, that's what minds do. The practice is in the returning. The analogy I use with this is like counting reps in the gym. When you are starting out, each time you notice your mind wandering and bring your attention back to breathing that's 1 rep! This helps to encourage you

when your mind wanders rather than thinking you are "doing it wrong". The more you practise the less frequently your mind will wander.
3. **Continue this process for your allotted time.**

This basic mindfulness meditation builds your "attention muscle" and creates space between your thoughts and your reactions. Over time, you'll notice yourself becoming less reactive and more responsive in your daily life.

There are many meditation styles: mindfulness, loving-kindness, body scan, transcendental, but don't get caught up in finding the "perfect" technique. The best meditation is the one you'll actually do consistently.

Visualisation: The Mental Rehearsal for Success

While meditation clears mental space, visualisation fills it with positive programming. Think of visualisation as meditation with intention, a powerful tool for aligning your subconscious with your conscious goals.

The Scientific Backbone of Visualisation

Dr Stephen Kosslyn, a pioneer in the field of mental imagery research, discovered through brain imaging studies that when you vividly imagine an activity, you activate many of the same neural networks that fire during the actual experience. This phenomenon, known as "functional equivalence", means your brain doesn't fully distinguish between vivid imagination and reality [70].

Chapter 10: Sustaining Your Transformation

This explains findings like the classic study by Australian psychologist Alan Richardson (1967), where researchers divided basketball players into three groups: [71]

- Group 1 practised free throws physically
- Group 2 visualised practising free throws
- Group 3 did not practice

After three months, Group 1 improved by 24%. Remarkably, Group 2 improved by 23%, nearly identical to physical practice, while Group 3 showed no improvement.

Neuroscientist Dr Andrew Newberg's research has shown that the neural patterns generated by vividly imagining an experience closely mirror those generated by the actual experience. This functional equivalence explains why visualisation can rewire neural pathways to support new behaviours and skills. [72]

Beyond Athletics: Visualisation in Medicine and Performance

Dr Charles Garfield, in his extensive study of peak performers across various fields, found that mental rehearsal was as important as physical rehearsal. World-class performers consistently created mental blueprints of their ideal performance, rehearsing these images repeatedly until they became second nature. [73]

Olympic gold medallist Michael Phelps attributed much of his success to visualisation: "I visualise the race from start to finish... I visualise the strokes, the walls, the turns, the finish, the strategy, all of it."

But visualisation isn't just for athletes. Dr Maxwell Maltz, a plastic surgeon, pioneered the use of mental rehearsal techniques and argued that visualisation could improve performance in professional settings [74]. Musicians using visualisation techniques showed neural changes identical to physical practice [75]. Public speakers who visualised successful presentations experienced reduced anxiety and improved performance [76].

Creating Visualisations that Rewire Your Brain

> **1. Create multi-sensory experiences.** McNorgan's research found that multi-sensory visualisation creates stronger neural patterns than visual imagery alone [77]. Don't just see your goal; hear, feel, smell and taste it.
>
> **2. Generate authentic emotion.** Neuroscientist Dr Antonio Damasio's research showed that emotion is the bridge between conscious and unconscious processing [78]. Feel the pride, joy, gratitude or excitement of achieving your goal. These emotions imprint the experience in your subconscious.
>
> **3. Use first-person perspective.** Research by Dr Melvin Slater showed that first-person visualisation (seeing through your own eyes) creates stronger neurological responses than third-person visualisation (seeing yourself from outside) [79]. Both have value, but the first-person perspective creates a stronger embodiment.
>
> **4. Include process, not just outcome.** Sports psychology research using the PETTLEP (Physical, Environment, Task, Timing, Learning, Emotion, and Perspective) model found

that athletes who visualised both the process (training, overcoming obstacles) and the outcome (victory) significantly outperformed those who only visualised the end result [80].

5. Practise at optimal times. Neuroscience research shows that your brain is most receptive to suggestion upon waking and before sleep, when you're naturally in alpha or theta states [81]. These are ideal times for visualisation practice.

Actor and comedian Jim Carrey famously wrote himself a check for $10 million for "acting services rendered", dated it years in the future and visualised it daily. Before the date on the check arrived, he had earned $10 million for his role in "Dumb and Dumber".

"Imagination is everything," Albert Einstein said. "It is the preview of life's coming attractions."

Visualisation works directly with your subconscious to create the identity, thought patterns and emotional states necessary for lasting change. It prepares your mind to recognise opportunities and solutions that align with your vision, making your desired future feel inevitable rather than merely possible.

Creating Systems for Sustainability

To truly sustain your transformation you need systems, reliable structures that support your growth regardless of how you feel on any given day.

Think of systems as the scaffolding that holds your new identity in place until it becomes self-supporting. Here are key systems to implement:

1. Environmental Design

Your environment shapes your behaviour more than willpower ever could. Restructure your physical space to support your goals.

Remember, your digital environment matters too. Curate your social media feeds, notification settings and screen time to align with your priorities.

2. Accountability Structures

We all have blind spots and moments of weakness. External accountability helps:

- **Accountability partners:** Find someone working towards similar goals and check in regularly.
- **Coaches or mentors:** Invest in professional guidance if possible.
- **Public commitments:** Share your intentions with those who will supportively hold you to them.
- **Tracking systems:** What gets measured improves. Track your key metrics.

3. Regular Review Rituals

Create structured times to assess your progress and recalibrate:

- **Daily reflection:** Brief evening journaling about what worked and what didn't.

- **Weekly planning:** Review the previous week and set intentions for the next.
- **Monthly deep dive:** Comprehensive review of goals, progress and needed adjustments.
- **Quarterly retreats:** Step back for bigger-picture evaluation and vision refinement.

These review rituals prevent drift and keep you consciously engaged with your transformation.

4. Emergency Response Plans

Even with the best systems, you'll face challenges. Plan for them:

- Identify your personal warning signs of regression.
- Create specific protocols for when you notice these signs.
- Develop a list of supportive resources to access during difficult times.
- Design environment modifications for high-stress periods.

Having these plans in place ensures that temporary setbacks don't become permanent reversals. You don't rise to the level of your goals; you fall to the level of your systems. If you want to change your results, don't focus on your outcomes. Focus on your processes.

The Compound Effect of Small Choices

Sustainability isn't about perfection; it's about consistency in the small choices that ultimately define your life.

The mathematics of transformation are elegantly simple: small, consistent actions compound into extraordinary results over time.

This principle proved transformational for Dmitri, who had struggled for years with a goal that seemed impossible until he changed his approach.

Dmitri stared at the blank document on his laptop screen, cursor blinking mockingly in the white void. Chapter 1. Again. For three years, he'd started his novel dozens of times, riding waves of inspiration that inevitably crashed against the rocks of "real life". His desk drawer was a graveyard of abandoned beginnings, brilliant first chapters that led nowhere and character sketches for stories that never found their voice.

The pattern was always the same: a burst of creative fire would strike, usually at 2 AM or during a boring commute. He'd race home, fingers flying across the keyboard for hours, convinced this time would be different. Then work would intrude, or social obligations or simple exhaustion, and the momentum would die. By the time he returned to the story, the magic had evaporated, leaving only inadequate words that felt foreign and forced.

"Maybe I'm not actually a writer," he'd think, watching real authors promote their published works on social media. "Maybe I'm just someone who likes the idea of being a writer." The manuscript in his head was brilliant: complex, moving, important. The scattered fragments on his hard drive were embarrassing evidence of his limitations.

The breakthrough came from the most unlikely source: a conversation with his neighbour about marathon training. "I don't run 26 miles in practice," she explained. "I run three miles every day, no matter what. Rain, shine, hangover, promotion at work,

Chapter 10: Sustaining Your Transformation

doesn't matter. Three miles, every single day. The marathon takes care of itself."

What if writing worked the same way? Instead of waiting for inspiration or perfect conditions, what if he committed to writing 500 words every day, regardless of quality or motivation? The idea felt both revolutionary and terrifying. Some days those words would be garbage, but garbage was still progress.

The first week was torture. He'd stare at the screen for forty minutes to produce two decent paragraphs and 300 words of what felt like literary debris. But he showed up. The second week was slightly easier. By the fourth week, something remarkable had happened: the story began to find its own momentum. Characters started surprising him. Plot threads wove together without conscious effort.

Six months later, Dmitri typed "The End" on a complete first draft. It wasn't perfect (first drafts never are) but it existed. The novel that had haunted him for three years was real, born not from inspiration but from the simple, unglamorous act of showing up every day with 500 words. He'd discovered that consistency was more powerful than brilliance and that small daily actions compound into extraordinary results.

These stories now have the emotional depth, vivid details and compelling narrative tension needed to serve as powerful proof points for the concepts while maintaining an appropriate length for the book's educational focus.

Dmitri's journey illustrates that sustainability isn't about perfection; it's about consistency in the small choices that ultimately define your life. Every positive choice you make, whether it's writing 500 words, taking a brief walk or following through on a commitment, adds another deposit into your transformation account.

Creating a Life Worth Sustaining

There's one final element to sustainability that's rarely discussed: creating a life that's genuinely worth sustaining.

Many people focus so intently on discipline and willpower that they forget to build a life they actually enjoy. Sustainability requires that your new patterns bring you genuine fulfilment, not just achievement.

Ask yourself:

- Does my transformed life include joy?
- Have I created space for play and creativity?
- Are my relationships deeper and more meaningful?
- Does my daily experience include moments of flow and engagement?
- Am I living from my values, not just my goals?

A sustainable transformation isn't just about becoming "better"; it's about becoming more authentically yourself. The goal isn't perfection but wholeness.

Chapter 10: Sustaining Your Transformation

The Journey Continues

As we near the end of this book, I want to acknowledge that transformation isn't a linear path. You'll have days of profound clarity and days of confusion. You'll experience breakthroughs and backslides. This is normal and human.

What matters most is your commitment to the journey itself, your willingness to get back up when you fall, to adjust course when needed and to continue growing despite setbacks.

Remember that your transformation isn't just for you. As you evolve, you impact everyone around you. Your growth creates ripples that extend far beyond what you can see. This is perhaps the greatest motivation for sustainability, recognising that your personal transformation is also your greatest contribution to others.

In the next chapter, we'll explore how to share your transformation in ways that inspire and elevate those around you, creating a positive cycle of change that extends far beyond yourself.

Chapter Summary

- **The framework for lasting change** requires alignment across identity, thoughts, emotions, actions and environment.
- **Energy overcomes entropy:** Without consistent attention, all systems (including your transformation) move towards disorder.
- **Meditation rewires your brain:** Research shows that meditation creates physical changes in brain structure and function, shifting you from beta to alpha and theta states.
- **Visualisation creates neural pathways:** When you vividly imagine success with all your senses, your brain creates the same neural connections as actual experience.
- **Systems ensure sustainability:** Create environmental, accountability, review and emergency-response systems.
- **Small choices compound:** Consistent 1% improvements lead to massive transformation over time.
- **Create a life worth sustaining:** Ensure your transformation includes joy, meaning and authenticity.

Your transformation is worth protecting. Give it the daily attention it deserves and it will continue to unfold in ways you can't yet imagine

Chapter 10: Sustaining Your Transformation

REFLECTION QUESTIONS

1. What changes have you successfully sustained in the past? What made these transformations lasting while others faded?
2. How do you typically respond when you encounter resistance or setbacks in your growth journey?
3. What systems could you create to support your ongoing transformation when motivation naturally wanes?

PRACTICAL EXERCISES

1. Energy Source Inventory

- For each type of energy, assess your current practices:
    - Physical energy: Sleep, nutrition, movement
    - Emotional energy: Positive relationships, gratitude, purpose
    - Mental energy: Focus, mindfulness, learning
    - Spiritual energy: Connection to something larger than yourself
    - Social energy: Supportive relationships
- Identify one area where investment would yield the greatest return
- Create a specific plan to enhance this energy source

2. Minimal Sustainability System

- Design a simple maintenance system for one area of transformation:
    - Daily practice: One 5-minute habit to maintain awareness

- - Environmental cue: A physical reminder in your space
  - Social support: One person to check in with weekly
  - Recovery protocol: A specific plan for when you get off track
- Keep this system intentionally small and sustainable rather than ambitious

3. Transformation Journal Start-up

- Create a dedicated journal for tracking your transformation journey
- Design a simple weekly review template with:
  - Three wins/successes to celebrate
  - One challenge and what you learned from it
  - Evidence of your new identity emerging
  - Focus area for the coming week
- Schedule 15 minutes each week for this reflection

Chapter 11: The Identity Wheel in Practice

Throughout our journey together, we've explored the fundamental concepts of the Identity Wheel and how it reveals the cyclical nature of personal growth. We've examined the architecture of the mind, delved into the power of identity, thoughts, beliefs and emotions, and discovered how to bridge the knowing-doing gap. We've learned to break negative confirmation loops, transform our reality through mindset and sustain our transformation through inevitable challenges.

Now it's time to bring all these insights together and explore how the Identity Wheel operates in various domains of your life. Because true transformation isn't compartmentalised – it's holistic, affecting every aspect of your existence. When you understand that the same universal principles apply whether you're building a career, nurturing relationships, improving your health or contributing to your community, you gain a powerful perspective that transcends circumstance and situation.

The Universal Wheel

Before we dive into specific applications, let's remind ourselves of a fundamental truth: the Identity Wheel operates with the same mechanics regardless of the domain. The process is always the same:

Your identity (who you believe yourself to be) determines your thoughts, which crystallise into beliefs. These thoughts and beliefs generate emotions, which drive your actions. Your actions create results, which then cycle back to either reinforce or challenge your original identity.

This wheel turns in your career just as it turns in your health journey. It operates in your intimate relationships just as it operates in your spiritual development. The principles remain consistent even as the specific content changes.

What changes isn't the process but the specific "I am" statements at the core of each domain's wheel. You might hold empowering identity statements in your career ("I am capable" or "I am resourceful") while simultaneously holding limiting ones in your health ("I am not athletic" or "I have bad genes").

The beauty of understanding the universal nature of the wheel is that once you master the process of transformation in one area, you can apply those same insights to any other area of your life. Success leaves clues, and the clues are remarkably consistent across domains.

Chapter 11: The Identity Wheel in Practice

The Identity Wheel in Relationships

Let's begin by examining how the Identity Wheel manifests in our relationships, arguably the area where our identity is most directly challenged and shaped [82]. The person you're in a relationship with isn't the person standing next to you – it's the person you believe yourself to be when you're with them.

Consider how a limiting identity statement like "I am unlovable" sets the entire wheel in motion within a relationship context. This core belief generates thoughts like, "My partner will eventually leave me" or "I need to hide my true self to be accepted". These thoughts create emotions of anxiety, insecurity and fear, which drive actions like jealousy, neediness or emotional withdrawal.

These actions inevitably create results that strain the relationship, leading to distance or conflict, which then cycles back to confirm the original identity: "See? I am unlovable." The wheel completes another turn, deepening the pattern with each rotation.

Kendra's story illustrates this cycle vividly. After a painful divorce, she carried an identity of "I am too much for people" into new relationships. This generated constant thoughts about overwhelming her partners, creating anxiety that led her to suppress her authentic self. She would hold back her opinions, downplay her achievements and avoid expressing her needs.

The results were predictable: shallow connections where she felt unseen and unappreciated, which only reinforced her belief that her full self was "too much" for others to handle. What Kendra couldn't see was that she wasn't creating evidence of being "too much"; she was creating evidence of the pain of being "too little" of herself.

The transformation began when Kendra recognised this pattern and intervened at the identity level. She started questioning the "I am too much" belief, looking for evidence that contradicted it. She began cautiously revealing more of herself in safe relationships, starting with close friends before moving to romantic connections.

"The first time I expressed a challenging opinion to someone I was dating and he responded with genuine interest rather than rejection was revolutionary," Kendra shared. "It cracked open the possibility that maybe, just maybe, I wasn't 'too much' after all."

Each positive interaction created a new data point that gradually shifted her identity. Over time, her new "I am worthy of being fully seen and accepted" identity generated different thoughts, emotions, actions and, ultimately, different relationship outcomes.

This same process applies to all relationships: romantic partnerships, friendships, family connections and professional relationships. The specific content changes, but the wheel turns with the same mechanics.

To apply the Identity Wheel to your relationships:

1. **Identify your core "I am" statements about yourself in relationship contexts.** Common limiting beliefs include "I am not enough", "I am responsible for others' happiness" or "I am destined to be abandoned".
2. **Notice the thoughts these identity statements generate.** How do you interpret your partner's actions?

Chapter 11: The Identity Wheel in Practice

What stories do you tell yourself about why people respond to you as they do?
3. **Observe the emotional states these thoughts create.** Do you cycle through anxiety, resentment or neediness? Do you find yourself emotionally shutting down?
4. **Track the actions that flow from these emotions.** Do you become controlling, people-pleasing, distant or confrontational?
5. **Honestly assess the results these actions create.** Are your relationships characterised by depth and authenticity, or by patterns of conflict, distance or co-dependency?

Once you've mapped this cycle, you can intervene at any point, though identity remains the most powerful entry point. By consciously choosing new "I am" statements about yourself in relationships and gathering evidence to support them, you set a new wheel in motion that can transform every connection in your life.

The Identity Wheel in Career and Business

Your professional life offers a particularly clear illustration of the Identity Wheel in action. The results you achieve in your career – the position you hold, the income you earn, the impact you make – are direct reflections of your professional identity and the wheel it sets in motion [83].

Consider Vedran, a talented software developer who carried the identity "I am a good technician but not leadership material." This core belief generated thoughts about staying in his lane and avoiding visibility. These thoughts created feelings of discomfort whenever leadership opportunities arose, which led him to decline projects that would put him in charge of others.

The results were predictable: despite his technical brilliance, Vedran remained in mid-level positions while watching less skilled colleagues advance to leadership roles. These results continually reinforced his original identity, creating a self-fulfilling prophecy that felt like objective reality rather than a pattern he was actively creating.

The transformation began when a perceptive mentor challenged Vedran's identity statement directly. "What if you're actually a potentially brilliant leader who simply hasn't developed those muscles yet?" she asked. This simple reframe, from fixed identity ("I am not leadership material") to growth identity ("I am developing my leadership capacity"), shifted everything.

With this new identity taking root, Vedran began to entertain different thoughts about leadership opportunities. Rather than seeing them as threats to avoid, he began viewing them as growth opportunities to embrace. These thoughts generated curiosity and excitement alongside the natural nervousness, which led him to take on small leadership responsibilities he would have previously declined.

Each small success created evidence that reinforced his new identity, gradually shifting the wheel in a positive direction. Within two years, Vedran was leading a team of developers and, more importantly, enjoying the experience.

The Identity Wheel operates just as powerfully for entrepreneurs and business owners. Your beliefs about what's possible in your

Chapter 11: The Identity Wheel in Practice

business, what you deserve to earn and who you are as a leader directly impact the actions you take and the results you create.

Many business owners unconsciously operate from limiting identities like "I am a small player in my industry" or "I am good at my craft but not at business". These identities generate thoughts about what's realistic or appropriate to charge, who you can approach as clients or how much you can delegate to others.

The resulting emotions, often anxiety about "overstepping" or imposter syndrome, lead to playing small through undercharging, avoiding high-value clients or micromanaging rather than delegating. The results of these actions then cycle back to confirm the original identity: "See? I am just a small player in this industry."

To apply the Identity Wheel to your career or business:

1. **Identify your professional identity statements.** What do you believe about yourself as a professional, leader or business owner?
2. **Examine the thoughts that flow from this identity.** What do you believe is possible or appropriate for someone like you in your field?
3. **Notice the emotions these thoughts generate.** Do you feel confident and expansive or constricted and anxious when thinking about professional growth?
4. **Track the actions (or inaction) these emotions drive.** Are you taking bold steps towards growth or playing it safe within your comfort zone?
5. **Honestly assess your professional results.** Are you creating the career trajectory, income and impact you desire?

The powerful intervention here is to consciously choose a new professional identity that aligns with your aspirations. Select an identity grounded in reality yet focused on growth and possibility rather than limitation.

For instance, shifting from "I am not business-minded" to "I am developing my business acumen daily" changes the entire wheel. The new identity generates thoughts about learning opportunities rather than fixed limitations, creating curiosity instead of resignation, which drives actions like investing in business education or finding mentors. These actions create improved business results, which reinforce the new growth-oriented identity.

The Identity Wheel in Health and Wellness

Perhaps nowhere is the Identity Wheel more vividly demonstrated than in our relationship with health and wellness. The results we experience in our physical well-being are direct reflections of the wheel set in motion by our health identity [84].

Consider Rafa, who carried the identity "I am not an athletic person" from childhood experiences of being picked last for sports teams. This core belief generated thoughts like "Exercise isn't for people like me" and "I'm just not built for fitness". These thoughts created feelings of discomfort and self-consciousness around physical activity, which led to avoidance of exercise and inconsistency with any programme he started.

The results were predictable: low energy, declining health markers and physical limitations that only reinforced his original identity: "See? I'm just not an athletic person."

Chapter 11: The Identity Wheel in Practice

What Rafa couldn't see was that his physical condition wasn't evidence of an inherent, unchangeable nature, it was the natural outcome of the wheel his identity had set in motion. His "non-athletic" identity created thoughts, emotions and actions that produced exactly the results that confirmed that identity.

Rafa's transformation began when he replaced his fixed identity ("I am not athletic") with a growth identity ("I am becoming more active every day"). This subtle shift (focusing on the process of becoming rather than a fixed state of being) changed everything.

The new identity generated thoughts about finding enjoyable ways to move rather than meeting some external standard of athleticism. These thoughts created curiosity rather than dread, which led to experimenting with different activities until he discovered a passion for hiking. The consistent movement improved his energy and physical confidence, creating evidence that reinforced his new identity as someone actively engaged in their health.

This same pattern applies to nutrition, sleep, stress management and all other aspects of health. Your identity statements about who you are in relation to these domains, "I am someone who needs comfort food when stressed" or "I am just not a morning person", set wheels in motion that create corresponding results.

To apply the Identity Wheel to your health:

1. **Identify your health identity statements.** What do you believe about yourself in relation to fitness, nutrition or overall wellness?

2. **Examine the thoughts these identities generate.** What do you tell yourself about what's possible or appropriate for someone like you?
3. **Notice the emotions these thoughts create.** Do you feel empowered or defeated when thinking about health improvements?
4. **Track the actions these emotions drive.** Are you consistently taking steps towards better health or remaining in familiar but unhealthy patterns?
5. **Honestly assess your health results.** Is your body functioning at its best potential, or are you experiencing limitations that don't serve you?

The intervention is to consciously choose a new health identity that focuses on growth and agency rather than limitation. Even small shifts like changing "I have bad genes" to "I am learning how to optimise my unique genetic blueprint" can transform your entire relationship with health.

The Wheel of Community and Contribution

While we often focus on the Identity Wheel's operation in personal domains like relationships, career and health, it's equally powerful in understanding our connection to broader communities and our contribution to the world [85].

Your identity statements about who you are in relation to your community, "I am someone who makes a difference" or conversely "I am too small to matter", set wheels in motion that create corresponding impacts.

Chapter 11: The Identity Wheel in Practice

Consider Elena, who carried the identity "I am too insignificant to affect real change" when thinking about social and environmental issues she cared about. This belief generated thoughts like "My actions are just a drop in the ocean" and "What's the point of trying when the problems are so vast?" These thoughts created feelings of hopelessness and resignation, which led to inaction on issues she genuinely cared about.

The results were predictable: no positive impact on the causes important to her, which only reinforced her original identity: "See? I really can't make a difference."

Elena's transformation began when she shifted to the identity "I am one person whose actions combine with others to create change." This seemingly subtle distinction, from isolated ineffectiveness to part of a collective impact, changed everything about how she engaged with her community.

This new identity generated thoughts about finding manageable ways to contribute rather than solving entire problems alone. These thoughts created feelings of empowerment and connection, which led to joining local environmental initiatives and making sustainable changes in her own life. Each small action created evidence of her ability to contribute meaningfully, reinforcing her new identity as someone who makes a difference as part of a larger whole.

This pattern applies whether you're contributing to family traditions, neighbourhood initiatives, professional communities or global causes. Your identity statements about your place and purpose within these groups directly impact the actions you take and the contribution you make.

To apply the Identity Wheel to your community engagement:

1. **Identify your community identity statements.** How do you see yourself in relation to the groups and causes you care about?
2. **Examine the thoughts these identities generate.** What do you believe about your capacity to contribute meaningfully?
3. **Notice the emotions these thoughts create.** Do you feel connected and empowered or isolated and insignificant?
4. **Track the actions these emotions drive.** Are you actively engaging with your communities or remaining passive on the sidelines?
5. **Honestly assess your impact.** Are you creating the ripple effects that align with your values?

The intervention is to consciously choose an identity that acknowledges both your individual significance and your connection to something larger. This balanced perspective, neither inflating nor diminishing your importance, creates a wheel of contribution that benefits both you and your communities.

Integrating the Wheels: The Whole-Life Approach

While we've examined how the Identity Wheel operates in different domains, the most powerful application comes from recognising that these aren't truly separate wheels – they're aspects of a single, integrated life wheel [86].

The identity that drives your career doesn't exist in isolation from the identity that shapes your relationships. The thoughts that influence your health affect your community engagement. The

Chapter 11: The Identity Wheel in Practice

emotions that impact your family life flow into your professional interactions.

This integration is both a challenge and an opportunity. The challenge is that limitation in one domain can bleed into others, creating broader patterns of constraint. If you carry a fundamental identity of "I am not enough" in your core sense of self this will manifest in each domain we've discussed, though perhaps in different forms.

You can't have a new life with an old identity. That's like redecorating a house when what you really need is to renovate.

The opportunity, however, is that transformation in one area can create positive momentum in others. When you experience the power of shifting your identity in your health journey, for example, you gain insights and confidence that can be applied to your career or relationships.

Thomas experienced this integrated transformation firsthand. He began with a focus on his physical health, shifting from "I am someone who can't stick with anything" to "I am building consistency one day at a time". As he accumulated evidence of his consistency through a modest but unbroken exercise routine, he noticed this new identity beginning to influence other domains.

"Once I proved to myself I could show up consistently for my health, I started to wonder where else I might apply this new self-image," Thomas shared. "I began approaching work projects with the same day-by-day consistency, and even my communication with my partner became more reliable. It was like unlocking one door opened access to many rooms I hadn't been able to enter before."

This is the power of an integrated approach to the Identity Wheel. Rather than compartmentalising transformation, you can leverage insights from each domain to create a cohesive, empowered identity that expresses itself across your entire life.

Teaching the Identity Wheel to Others

As you experience transformation through understanding and applying the Identity Wheel, you may feel inspired to share these insights with others: perhaps your children, team members, friends or clients. This is a natural extension of growth; as we evolve, we want to help others do the same.

The key to effectively teaching the Identity Wheel lies in embodiment rather than mere explanation. People are far more influenced by what you do than by what you articulate. When others witness your transformation: seeing the tangible changes in how you respond to challenges, make decisions and create results, they naturally become curious about the principles guiding your evolution.

When that curiosity arises, consider these approaches:

1. **Begin with personal stories rather than theory.** Share specific examples of how you recognised a limiting pattern in your life and how understanding the wheel helped you transform it. Concrete examples are always more compelling than abstract concepts.

2. **Meet people where they are.** Not everyone is ready to examine their core identity or deep-seated beliefs. Sometimes beginning with the action-results connection is more accessible, helping others see how specific behaviours create predictable outcomes before diving into the thought and identity patterns behind those behaviours.
3. **Focus on one domain that matters to them.** If someone is struggling with health challenges, start by applying the wheel to that specific context rather than attempting to address their entire life at once. Success in one area creates openness to broader applications.
4. **Emphasise intervention points rather than perfect understanding.** People don't need to master the entire concept to begin experiencing benefits. Help them identify one point where they can intervene in their current patterns, whether at the identity, thought, emotion or action level, and support them in that specific shift.
5. **Practise patience and non-judgement.** Remember that each person's journey unfolds at its own pace. What seems obvious to you now may have taken years of your own experience to fully grasp. Allow others the same grace you've needed on your path.

When teaching children the Identity Wheel, simplification is essential but beware of oversimplification. Even young children can understand that how they think about themselves influences how they feel, which affects what they do and what happens as a result. Use age-appropriate examples they can relate to, like how thinking "I'm bad at maths" makes them feel worried, which might lead them to rush through homework, resulting in mistakes that seem to "prove" they're bad at maths.

Teaching through embodiment applies especially to parenting. Children absorb your way of being far more than your words of instruction. When they see you pause in a challenging moment to choose a different thought or response, they're learning the principles of the wheel without needing its terminology.

The Win-the-Day Approach in Every Domain

Throughout our journey, we've explored the power of the "Win-the-Day" methodology – focusing on daily actions that compound over time rather than becoming overwhelmed by distant goals. This approach is universally applicable across all life domains and provides a practical framework for implementing the Identity Wheel in everyday life.

In your career, winning the day might mean completing five high-impact tasks on your Power List that move key projects forward, regardless of whether you "feel" motivated. In your relationships, it might mean being fully present for one meaningful conversation without digital distractions. In your health, it might mean following through on your planned movement and nutrition choices for just today, without worrying about tomorrow.

The beauty of this approach is that it makes the abstract principles of the Identity Wheel immediately actionable. You're not trying to transform your entire identity, thought patterns and emotional responses at once, you're simply focusing on winning today in specific, concrete ways.

Over time, these daily wins create evidence that challenges limiting identities and supports empowering ones. Each day you follow through on your Power List, you build evidence against "I

Chapter 11: The Identity Wheel in Practice

am someone who can't finish what I start" and for "I am someone who does what needs to be done." Each day you show up fully for one meaningful conversation, you create evidence against "I am too busy for deep connection" and for "I am present for what matters most".

This day-by-day approach aligns perfectly with the Identity Wheel because it recognises that sustainable transformation isn't about dramatic overnight changes; it's about consistent rotation of the wheel in a positive direction until a new pattern becomes your default.

The Chinese Bamboo Tree: A Metaphor for Transformation

As we integrate the Identity Wheel into every domain of life, the story of the Chinese bamboo tree offers a powerful metaphor for the transformation process. This remarkable tree shows virtually no visible growth for the first four years after planting, just a tiny shoot poking through the soil. Yet during this seemingly dormant period, the tree is developing an extensive root system beneath the ground. Then, in the fifth year, it suddenly shoots up 80 feet in just six weeks.

This growth pattern perfectly illustrates the reality of transformation through the Identity Wheel. When you begin consciously shifting your identity and thought patterns, the external results may not be immediately visible. You might feel that nothing is changing despite your consistent efforts, just like that farmer watering and tending a seemingly unresponsive shoot for years.

What you can't see, however, is the extensive "root system" being established in your subconscious mind. Each time you consciously choose a new identity statement, challenge a limiting thought, regulate an emotional response or take aligned action despite fear, you're strengthening these invisible roots.

Then, often when you least expect it, the external manifestation of your internal work suddenly becomes visible, sometimes dramatically so. Opportunities align, relationships transform, health improves and impact expands in ways that might seem sudden to outside observers but that you recognise as the natural outcome of your persistent inner work.

The bamboo tree metaphor reminds us of an essential truth about the Identity Wheel: transformation operates on its own timeline, not according to our expectations or demands. Some shifts in the wheel create immediate, visible results, while others build momentum invisibly before manifesting externally.

The farmer who understands the bamboo tree's growth pattern continues watering and tending the shoot not because of visible evidence but because of knowledge and faith in the process. Similarly, your understanding of the Identity Wheel allows you to continue your inner work with confidence even when external results aren't yet visible, trusting in the natural unfolding of transformation.

The Universal Principles at Work

As we conclude our exploration of the Identity Wheel in practice, it's worth reflecting on the universal principles that operate across all domains of life. These principles aren't arbitrary or random;

they're expressions of how reality itself functions, as consistent and reliable as physics or mathematics.

The principle of identity determines possibility: who you believe yourself to be defines the boundaries of what you can experience and achieve.

The principle of thought creates direction: what you consistently think about shapes the course of your attention and energy.

The principle of emotion generates fuel: how you feel determines the quality and quantity of energy available for action.

The principle of action produces evidence: what you do creates tangible results that either confirm or challenge your existing beliefs.

The principle of reflection enables evolution: your awareness and interpretation of results determine whether the wheel continues its current pattern or shifts in a new direction.

These principles operate whether you're conscious of them or not, just as gravity functions regardless of your belief in it. The difference is that when you understand these principles and work with them intentionally, you move from being a passive subject of their influence to becoming an active participant in your own evolution.

This is the ultimate promise of the Identity Wheel: not a life free from challenges or a path of perpetual ease, but the profound empowerment that comes from understanding the mechanics of your own experience. With this understanding, you're no longer at the mercy of unconscious patterns, you're the conscious creator of your life across every domain.

The Journey Continues

As our formal exploration of the Identity Wheel concludes, remember that your journey with these principles is just beginning. True mastery comes not from intellectual understanding but from lived application, from moments of conscious choice in the laboratory of daily life.

There will be times when you revert to old patterns, when limiting identities reassert themselves, when negative thought spirals capture your attention, when challenging emotions overwhelm your awareness or when habitual actions override your conscious intentions. This is not failure; it's simply the nature of being human, of rewiring neural pathways that have been established over decades.

Each time you notice these old patterns, you have a new opportunity to intervene in the wheel, to make a different choice, to set a new cycle in motion. With practice, these interventions become more natural, more immediate and more effective, gradually transforming your default settings across every domain of life.

The Identity Wheel is not a destination to reach but a journey to embrace; one that unfolds uniquely for each person while operating on the same universal principles. As you continue applying these insights in your relationships, career, health and community engagement, you'll discover new dimensions of the wheel and fresh applications of its wisdom.

Chapter 11: The Identity Wheel in Practice

The wheel keeps turning, always. Your power lies not in stopping its motion but in consciously directing its course – one thought, one emotion, one action, one day at a time.

Chapter Summary

- **The Identity Wheel operates universally** across all domains of life, from relationships to career to health to community engagement.

- **Domain-specific identity statements** determine the patterns that unfold in each area of your life, though the wheel's mechanics remain consistent.

- **Transformation in one domain** can create positive momentum that influences other areas through integrated identity shifts.

- **Teaching the Identity Wheel to others** is most effective through embodiment and personalised application rather than abstract explanation.

- **The Win-the-Day approach** provides a practical framework for implementing the wheel's principles through daily actions that compound over time.

- **The Chinese bamboo tree metaphor** illustrates how internal transformation often precedes visible external results, developing strong "roots" before dramatic growth.

- **Universal principles operate consistently** across all domains, empowering conscious participation in your own evolution.

Chapter 11: The Identity Wheel in Practice

REFLECTION QUESTIONS

1. How do you see the Identity Wheel operating across different domains of your life? Where is it turning most effectively, and where is it stuck?
2. What common identity themes do you notice across various life areas (relationships, career, health, community)?
3. How might shifting your identity in one domain create positive ripple effects in others?

PRACTICAL EXERCISES

1. Domain Integration Map

- Draw your own Identity Wheel diagram
- Around it, draw four circles labelled: Relationships, Career, Health, Community
- In each domain, note your current identity, dominant thoughts, prevalent emotions and typical actions
- Look for patterns, connections and contradictions across domains
- Identify one identity shift that might positively influence multiple domains

2. Teaching Through Example

- Select one Identity Wheel concept that has been most meaningful to you
- Write a brief, concrete example of how you've applied this concept in your life

- Consider how you might naturally share this insight with someone else through your actions rather than abstract explanation
- Practise embodying this understanding in a way that might inspire curiosity in others

3. Next Steps Planning

- Based on everything you've learned through this book:
    - What is your highest priority for transformation?
    - What daily practice will support this transformation?
    - What environment modifications will reinforce your new identity?
    - What further resources or support would accelerate your journey?
- Create a specific plan for deepening your understanding and application of the Identity Wheel concept.

Chapter 12: Transformation Stories

The four stories that follow represent a carefully selected cross-section of people who have applied the Identity Wheel framework to create lasting change in their lives. These accounts were chosen not because they represent perfect outcomes or extraordinary circumstances, but because they illustrate the universal principles at work across different ages, backgrounds and challenges.

Mollie, a 24-year-old musician, demonstrates how the Identity Wheel operates when limiting beliefs become so deeply embedded that they feel like unchangeable facts. Her story reveals how someone can break free from cycles of self-destructive behaviour by recognising the difference between their authentic self and the negative identity they've constructed.

Sean, a university graduate entering the professional world, shows how the Identity Wheel manifests in career development and the transition to adulthood. His experience illustrates that impostor syndrome isn't really about competence but about identity, and how shifting that identity can unlock previously inaccessible levels of performance.

Kelly, a senior HR professional, exemplifies how even accomplished individuals can remain trapped by limiting beliefs rooted in their past. Her story demonstrates that success in one area of life doesn't automatically eliminate identity limitations in others, and how the same framework applies whether you're starting your career or leading others.

Andy, an entrepreneur and father of five, represents perhaps the most challenging scenario: how the Identity Wheel operates during crisis when external circumstances seem to validate our worst fears about ourselves. His story shows that transformation is possible even when life genuinely falls apart, because the quality of our internal experience isn't determined by our external circumstances.

As you read these accounts, notice several key patterns:

The Universal Mechanics: Despite vastly different life circumstances, each person's challenges follow the same Identity Wheel pattern. Limiting "I am" statements generate thoughts, which create emotions, which drive actions, which produce results that confirm the original identity.

Multiple Intervention Points: Each person found their breakthrough by intervening at different points in the wheel. Mollie focused heavily on emotional regulation and boundary setting; Sean worked primarily on professional identity and daily habits; Kelly discovered the power of journaling to separate thoughts from facts; Andy learnt to distinguish catastrophic thinking from reality.

The Role of Daily Practice: None of these transformations happened through single insights or dramatic moments. Each person developed daily practices such as journaling, gratitude, exercise and meditation that gradually shifted their default patterns.

Resistance and Return: Notice how each person encountered resistance from their old identity, moments when familiar patterns reasserted themselves. The difference wasn't the absence of challenges but their response to them.

The Compound Effect: Small shifts in identity created ripple effects across multiple life domains. Improving self-worth enhanced professional performance; developing boundaries strengthened relationships; building consistency in one area transferred to others.

These stories aren't included to suggest that transformation is easy or guaranteed. Change requires genuine commitment, consistent practice and often professional support. Rather, they're here to demonstrate that the principles explored throughout this book operate reliably across different personalities, circumstances and challenges.

Each person's journey is unique, but the underlying mechanics are universal. As you read their accounts, consider how similar patterns might be operating in your own life and which intervention points might offer the greatest leverage for your own transformation.

Remember what I shared in Chapter 1: your identity isn't your destiny; it's your starting point. These four individuals discovered this truth in their own unique ways, and their experiences offer both hope and practical insight into how you might apply the same principles to create your own breakthrough.

Mollie's Story: Breaking Free from the Cycle of Self-Doubt

Mollie's alarm would go off each morning, but instead of getting up, she'd reach for her phone and disappear into endless social media scrolling. Hours would pass watching other musicians succeed while a familiar narrative played in her head: "I'm not good enough. I'm damaged. I'm worthless."

What she didn't realise was that she had become addicted to these feelings.

"I didn't realise how addicted I was to feeling bad about myself; it was like a frenzy in my mind," Mollie reflects. "I was subconsciously looking for something to sway my mood and determine how I spent the rest of my day, stuck in bed in a loop."

This was Mollie's reality two years ago: a talented musician trapped in repetitive cycles of misery, self-medicating to numb the pain and making decisions that proved all the terrible things she believed about herself.

The Prison of Negative Identity

Chapter 12: Transformation Stories

The "I am" statements that ran Mollie's life read like a prosecutor's closing argument: "I am stupid." "I am not worthy of love." "I am damaged." "I am worthless."

These weren't occasional negative thoughts – they formed the core of her identity. Her belief that she was "worthless" generated thoughts focused on everything wrong with her life. These thoughts created feelings of depression and inadequacy, which drove actions like people-pleasing, self-medicating and avoiding opportunities.

The results were predictable: toxic relationships, unfulfilling musical projects taken on just to please others and a persistent sense of failing at life. Each disappointing outcome cycled back to confirm her original identity: "See? I really am worthless."

"I was subconsciously doing all of these things to myself to prove myself right about everything that was wrong with me," she explains. "It seemed better to be correct and fail rather than risk disappointing myself."

The Breakthrough: Seeing the Pattern

Mollie's transformation began with small revelations that gradually illuminated the prison she had built around herself.

The Gratitude Awakening "I couldn't believe how simple this idea was, but also how much I was lacking this in my life," Mollie recalls about discovering gratitude practice. "When I was in a bad headspace, I found it extremely hard to acknowledge anything good about my life. It started to ring alarm bells about how much of an enemy my mind was."

This wasn't just positive thinking – it was recognising how her mind actively filtered out evidence that contradicted her negative self-image.

The Boundary Revolution Perhaps more transformative was Mollie's discovery that she could set boundaries. "I didn't feel I could be a good person and set boundaries to protect myself," she admits. "It was eye-opening to realise how much of a people pleaser this had made me, and how allowing people to inflict their own boundaries on my decisions demonstrated such a lack of self-respect."

The Structure Solution "My routine was all over the place before, and every bad day backed onto the next day, making it feel endless," Mollie explains. "I realised how important structure and routine were to keep me focused, put my headspace back on track and ground me."

The Tools That Broke the Cycle

Mollie discovered that transformation required more than just wanting to change, it required specific tools and daily practices.

"Journaling morning and night was a great way to reflect on my day and enhanced my goal-setting ability, gratitude and being intentional," she explains. "Being able to see my day on a page gave me the ability to see things more rationally, understand what my triggers were and recognise the early warning signs."

This became her secret weapon for breaking thought patterns, allowing her to observe emotional storms with clarity rather than being swept away by them.

She developed routines including journaling, exercise, time in nature and maintaining meaningful relationships. "I ensure I'm doing all the things I need to keep my mind and body healthy, which helps me maintain boundaries and have independent time to recharge."

The Transformation: A New Life

Within three months, Mollie experienced "a complete new lease on life".

"I am now involved in multiple projects and bands that align with my goals, receiving opportunities I had never been exposed to before. This is a huge shift from taking on projects I wasn't passionate about to please others."

"My income has increased through performing at venues and events I had always aspired to play, rather than settling for opportunities I thought I deserved and underpricing myself."

"After losing trust through poor relationships and building emotional barriers out of fear, I am now in a happy and secure relationship – something I didn't believe was possible for myself."

"The majority of my time is spent dedicating it to my goals. I don't waste time doom scrolling or lying in bed in a mental frenzy of bad thoughts about myself. I care less about how I'm perceived and live far more authentically than I ever have."

When Old Patterns Try to Return

When Mollie joined a third band and faced familiar feelings of inadequacy, she caught herself in the old pattern. "It was through journaling that I was able to identify my irrational thoughts and see what I was doing to make these situations worse – how I was slowly shifting back into the mentality of a victim."

The difference was striking. "Prior to this work, I would have quit and begun down a path of feeling inadequate and unworthy of opportunities, but this didn't happen. I was able to identify the issues and get back on track."

A Message of Hope

"Two years ago, I felt like I was stuck in a place that was inescapable," she reflects. "I never imagined I'd be where I am today, actually living again. What I didn't realise then was how something as simple as following frameworks and sticking to good habits and routines could transform every part of my life."

Her message to others is direct: "Don't give up. Change can happen, even when it feels impossible."

Sean's Story: From Graduate Impostor to Six-Figure Success

Sean stared at his laptop screen on his first day at the recruitment firm, surrounded by colleagues who seemed to effortlessly navigate client calls and candidate conversations. Fresh out of university, he felt like an actor who'd wandered onto the wrong film set.

"I felt like I was constantly waiting to be found out," Sean reflects. "Like someone would eventually realise I didn't belong there and send me packing."

Chapter 12: Transformation Stories

This was Sean's reality as a new graduate: academically capable but emotionally unprepared for professional life, trapped in cycles of self-doubt that kept him small.

The Prison of "Not Enough"

Sean's internal dialogue was a constant stream of inadequacy: "I don't know enough." "I am too young." "I am not as good as others." "I am not ready for the real world."

These weren't occasional moments of self-doubt – they formed the foundation of how he saw himself. His core belief that he "wasn't ready" generated thoughts focused on everything he lacked compared to his colleagues. These thoughts created emotions of anxiety and inadequacy, which drove actions like avoiding speaking up in meetings, saying yes to every difficult placement to prove his worth and developing poor spending habits as comfort.

The results were predictable: staying invisible at work, financial stress, neglecting his health and relationships and a persistent sense that everyone else had figured out "adulting" except him. Each disappointing outcome cycled back to confirm his original identity: "See? I really don't know what I'm doing."

The Breakthrough: Recognising the Pattern

Sean's transformation began in May, several months into working with Dan, when something fundamental shifted.

"The biggest breakthrough was understanding that my identity was literally creating my reality," Sean explains. "I started to see how my belief that I 'wasn't ready' was actually keeping me from becoming ready."

Working with Dan, Sean began tracing where his limiting mindset originated and started setting realistic boundaries and expectations. "Instead of trying to be perfect straight away, I focused on becoming 1% better consistently."

"I realised that my bad habits weren't character flaws – they were just patterns I could change," Sean reflects. "Once I saw them as systems rather than personal failures, everything became manageable."

The Tools That Built Confidence

"Rather than trying to become the perfect recruiter overnight, Dan helped me break down where my insecurities came from and set boundaries around what I could realistically achieve each week," Sean explains.

Sean began consciously challenging his "I am" statements, replacing "I don't know enough" with "I'm learning quickly" and "I'm too young" with "I bring fresh perspective."

"I finally sorted out my gym routine and started seeing real gains. It's amazing how much easier it is to take care of yourself when you believe you're worth it."

The Transformation: A New Professional Identity

Within four months, Sean experienced what he describes as entering "a completely new stage of life".

"I went from hiding in meetings to actively contributing ideas. I stopped seeing my age and experience level as disadvantages."

"I had my first £35,000 month in May, and I'm on track for £100,000 this year. The financial success came naturally once I stopped operating from a place of 'not enough'."

"My relationships improved dramatically. I moved to London, my dating life became much stronger, and I developed genuine financial security."

"Life feels fantastic now. I have good relationships, a strong dating life and financial security – all whilst navigating a major life change like moving to London."

Sustaining the Change

"I see this work like going to the gym – it doesn't really end," Sean explains. "The difference is that now I have the tools to handle challenges when they come up, rather than being derailed by them."

When new situations trigger old patterns of impostor syndrome, Sean now has a framework for recognising and shifting them quickly, rather than spiralling into weeks of self-doubt.

A Message of Hope

"If you're feeling like an impostor in your first job, know that it's not actually about your age or experience level," Sean advises. "It's about the identity you're operating from. Once you understand that your thoughts about yourself are creating your reality, you can start consciously choosing better thoughts.

Kelly's Story: From Council Estate to Confident Leader

Kelly sat in the boardroom, surrounded by colleagues discussing a major organisational change. As a senior HR professional, she should have felt confident contributing to the conversation. Instead, a familiar voice whispered in her head: "You're a shit kid from a council estate with an accent. Everyone thinks you are a show off. People are bored and tired of you."

The irony wasn't lost on her. Here she was, someone whose job was to support others' development and wellbeing, yet she couldn't silence the internal critic that told her she didn't belong in that room.

The Prison of Perceived Inadequacy

Kelly's internal dialogue was brutal: "You're not enough." "You're not worthy." "No one thinks you are good." "People don't like you, they just tolerate you." "Nobody really cares about you."

These weren't just passing thoughts of self-doubt. They formed the foundation of an identity that kept her trapped in cycles of overcompensation and emotional exhaustion.

"I was earning my worth," Kelly reflects. "I felt like love was conditional on what I did for other people." This belief drove her to work longer hours, take on more responsibilities and constantly prove herself worthy of her position. Yet no amount of external validation could silence the voice that told her she was "only one mistake away from throwing away everything I had achieved".

Chapter 12: Transformation Stories

"I was waiting for someone to be malicious and tell me how bad I am or how rubbish I am and I am not 'all that!'" The anticipation of criticism became almost worse than actual feedback, creating a state of hypervigilance that left her mentally drained.

The Doom Spiral Pattern

Kelly's struggles manifested in what she calls "doom spirals". When challenges arose, her mind would cascade into negative thinking that seemed to feed on itself.

"When I was in a doom spiral or in my negative thoughts and feelings, I felt completely overwhelmed," she explains. One particular incident crystallised this pattern – she found herself in a situation where she felt unsupported and distrustful of those around her.

In the past, this would have sent her into a familiar spiral: working excessive hours, second-guessing every decision and desperately seeking validation from others. The emotional toll was exhausting.

The Breakthrough: Finding Truth Through Words

Kelly's transformation began with a simple but powerful discovery: journaling. When that familiar situation of feeling unsupported arose, Kelly tried something different. Instead of immediately reacting, she wrote down exactly what she was experiencing:

"Today I am feeling anxious and unstable because I think X is all going to go wrong and I will be blamed and shamed. I will be humiliated and people will be happy that I came undone."

Then came the crucial step, writing the truth:

"I am feeling anxious and unstable because in the past, in similar situations, I have not received the support I deserved or required. My body is remembering this pain and trying to warn me. Thank you, body for giving me this warning. I am not in the same situation as before."

She would then write about the things in her current situation that were different and supportive.

The Power of Perspective Shift

This process revealed something profound: her anxiety wasn't evidence of current danger but her body's way of protecting her based on past experiences. "Thank you, body for giving me this warning" became a revolutionary reframe.

Instead of seeing her anxiety as weakness or evidence that she didn't belong, Kelly learnt to see it as her nervous system trying to keep her safe.

"I was then able to decide the action I took from a position of awareness rather than a negative thought pattern fuelled by emotion," Kelly explains.

Kelly also discovered the power of focusing on "bigger, more meaningful goals rather than just tactical ones". Instead of being driven by fear-based goals like "don't make mistakes," she began focusing on purpose-driven goals like "create environments where people can thrive".

Chapter 12: Transformation Stories

The Ongoing Journey

Kelly's transformation wasn't a one-time event but an ongoing practice. "I guess it was a work in progress over a year, and it continues!" she reflects.

The results speak for themselves: "I don't spiral as much, panic or become depressed as quickly. I have a better perspective on work challenges and this has had a positive impact on my mental health."

Kelly learnt that transformation doesn't mean never experiencing difficult emotions again – it means developing the tools to work with them skilfully when they arise.

A Message of Hope

Kelly's story demonstrates that even high-achieving professionals can be trapped by limiting beliefs rooted in their past. Her journey from a "shit kid from a council estate" (as her inner critic would say) to a confident senior leader wasn't about denying her roots but about refusing to let her past define her potential.

Through consistent practice and the courage to write down both her fears and her truth, Kelly transformed from someone who was "earning her worth" to someone who knew her inherent value.

Andy's Story:
From Business Collapse to Authentic Success

Andy lay awake at 3 AM, his mind racing with the same catastrophic thoughts that had kept him sleepless for weeks. The million-pound mortgage brokerage business he'd built over four and a half years was gone. The partnership with his longtime colleague had imploded spectacularly. His income had vanished overnight, leaving him with five children, a wife, a mortgage and no clear path forward.

"I couldn't see a way out," Andy reflects. "I was catastrophising everything. My wife Laura was so worried about my mental state that she'd call me 15 minutes after I left for work just to make sure I hadn't pulled over and done something stupid."

This wasn't just business stress – this successful entrepreneur had reached a breaking point where dark thoughts had entered his mind, thoughts he'd never experienced before.

The Prison of Catastrophic Thinking

Andy's internal dialogue had become a relentless cycle of worst-case scenarios. His core identity had shifted to "I've lost everything" and "I'm a failure who's destroyed my family's security." This belief generated thoughts that spiralled into elaborate disaster predictions: they'd lose the house, the children would suffer, he'd never recover professionally.

These thoughts created overwhelming emotions of anxiety, shame and hopelessness, which drove destructive behaviours: heavy drinking to numb the pain, isolating himself from family and friends and complete avoidance of addressing the practical realities he needed to face.

The results were predictable: his mental health deteriorated further, his relationship with his wife and children became strained, and he remained paralysed rather than taking any constructive action. Each day of inaction seemed to confirm his worst fears: "See? I really can't handle this. I've ruined everything."

But Andy couldn't see that his suffering wasn't just caused by his circumstances – it was amplified by the way he was thinking about his circumstances.

The Reluctant First Step

Andy's transformation began with his wife Laura's intervention. Recognising the dangerous trajectory he was on, she insisted he attend a mindset event – something Andy dismissed as "woo-woo fairy fluffy" nonsense.

"I thought I'll go and sit down for an hour and a half, grit my teeth, get through it, and that'll keep her happy for another week while I try and work out what I'm going to do next," Andy recalls.

But something shifted during that event. "There were speakers talking about men's mental health and battles they'd been through. I could resonate with some of the stories and some of the thoughts people had shared – I'd had those same dark thoughts."

When Andy heard Daniel speak, something clicked. "You put it in a way where I just understood what you were saying. I came away with this weird feeling that I wanted to reach out and see if you could help me."

Despite having no income and uncertain finances, both Andy and Laura agreed that investing in coaching felt like the right decision.

The Breakthrough: Separating Thoughts from Facts

Andy's most significant breakthrough came from learning to distinguish between his thoughts and actual facts.

"I'd spent so long thinking about all the permutations of things that could happen that those thoughts became, in my head, a reality," Andy explains. "I would catastrophise them, which would send me into a downward spiral."

Through the coaching work, Andy developed the ability to pause when his mind began racing: "Now I'm able to go, 'Okay, so it's a thought. What out of that thought is a fact, and what am I just conjuring up in my head?'"

This wasn't about positive thinking or denial – it was about accuracy. "A lot of it was coming from paradigms, things that had been instilled in me for so long that in my head I believed they were truths when there was no truth behind them whatsoever."

Andy learned to ask himself crucial questions: "What has actually happened? What's in my control? What are the bits I can do something about?" This shift from rumination to genuine thinking was transformational.

Discovering False Beliefs About Confidence

Another major breakthrough involved examining Andy's belief that he "lacked confidence". Through careful questioning, this blanket statement unravelled completely.

Chapter 12: Transformation Stories

"You sat me down one day and said, 'Let's get into that. You run a business that's been really successful, you looked after staff and clients, you have five kids – so what exactly is it that you think you're not confident in?'"

This investigation revealed that Andy's supposed "lack of confidence" was actually rooted in one specific area, traceable to a prominent figure in his life who was narcissistic and had systematically undermined his self-belief for their own benefit.

"A lot of the misconceptions and beliefs and paradigms that I had, I can track back to that person," Andy explains. "It's only once you start to uncover that and get into it that you can start to see how your thinking has been heavily affected by things that are completely untrue."

The Tools That Created Change

Daily Journaling Practice: Despite initial resistance ("I never thought I'd say this because it's just not what I could have ever seen myself doing"), Andy became a "prolific journal writer", writing every morning and evening.

"For me, it's so important to be able to get down what's going on in my head. Quite often when I journal, I can correct the misleading thought pattern that I have. I'll write down 'Today I'm feeling crap because of this reason', but then I write out what's actually happened and what I can control. By the end of writing the journal, I've kind of fixed whatever was misfiring in my head."

Gratitude Practice: "The dreaded – and I rolled my eyes when you asked me to do it – gratitude practice," Andy admits. "I write down what I'm grateful for, the things that have happened through the day. That one's really good because it's finding the gratitude in the little things we normally overlook, which are actually really big things."

Core Values Alignment: Perhaps most importantly, Andy identified his authentic core values: consistency, commitment, determination, family and peace. These became his decision-making filter.

"I live my life by those core values now. When I wake up in the morning and don't want to go to the gym, which happens four or five times a week, I think, 'But consistency is your core value. How are you going to feel if you don't do it?'. I know if I don't do it, I'm going to hate myself because I haven't lived my life based on the person I want to be."

The Transformation: A Different Kind of Success

Within months of beginning the coaching programme, Andy's life had fundamentally changed – not through external circumstances improving, but through his internal transformation.

Professional Resilience: Andy started a new business from scratch. While challenges arose regularly, his response was completely different. "The wobbles last for 10 or 15 minutes now because I'm equipped with the tools. Once you've had that thought, you stop and go, 'I'm being an idiot. I've taken myself there based on absolutely no fact whatsoever. Let's get back to what are the facts, what I can control, and focus on those bits.'"

Chapter 12: Transformation Stories

Family Relationships Transformed: "My relationship, especially with the older kids, is a hundred times better than it's ever been because I'm present and genuinely interested. The kids say to me that I am a better role model to them now than I've ever been. I can't give them the money I used to, can't deck them out in designer clothes – but they don't care. They never wanted it anyway. They wanted me present."

Marriage Strengthened: The coaching work led to conversations Andy and Laura had never had before, including monthly check-ins where they discussed what was working and what needed improvement in their relationship. "Some of the things she said – I'd been doing things that upset her, but she would never have told me that before."

Internal Peace: "I'm probably the least in control of my life I've ever been from a financial and business perspective, but I feel more in control because I'm in control of me," Andy explains. "I don't get caught up in the ifs, buts and maybes. It's all about the now, controlling the things we can control as a family, enjoying the things we can enjoy."

When Old Patterns Return

Andy's transformation didn't eliminate challenges – it changed how he responds to them. "You're never going to stop the thoughts coming into your head. I can sometimes almost chuckle to myself when I've gone on this little journey of catastrophising for 20–25 minutes, then I stop and go, 'I'm being an idiot'."

The key difference is speed and self-awareness. Problems that used to derail him for days or weeks now get resolved within hours because he has the tools to separate facts from fears and focus on what he can actually control.

A Message of Hope

"What happened to me was the worst thing that's ever happened to me in my life, but I can genuinely sit here now and say it was the best thing that's ever happened to me," Andy reflects. "I don't think I would have ever committed to this work and taken it as seriously unless I'd hit rock bottom."

His advice to others considering similar work is direct: "The success is going to be wholly dependent on you. You can be given all the information in the world, but it's up to you to implement it, really understand it, believe it and live by it. You're only going to get out of it what you put in. But if you're prepared to commit, you will almost instantly see results."

Andy's story demonstrates that even successful entrepreneurs can find themselves trapped by unconscious thought patterns, and that sometimes our greatest breakdowns become the foundation for our greatest breakthroughs – not through external rescue, but through the courage to examine our own thinking and reclaim control over our internal world.

The 30-Day Identity Wheel Transformation Plan

One focused task per day. Complete in order for maximum impact or accelerate by doing multiple tasks in one sitting.

Week 1: See Your Current Pattern (Days 1–7)

"You cannot change what you cannot see."

Day 1: Choose Your Focus

Write down the ONE "I am..." statement that limits you most across multiple life areas. Not the biggest or scariest but the one you're actually ready to question. *Examples: "I am not good with money", "I am socially awkward", "I am not leadership material".*

Time: 10 minutes

Day 2: Find the Origin

The Identity Wheel

Write down when you first remember believing this about yourself. Who said it? What happened? What did this belief protect you from at the time?

Time: 15 minutes

Day 3: Map Your Wheel

For your limiting identity, complete this sentence 5 times: *"When I believe I am [limiting identity], I think..." "These thoughts make me feel..." "These feelings cause me to..." "These actions create results like..." "These results prove I am [limiting identity] because..."*

Time: 15 minutes

Day 4: Count the Cost

List 5 specific opportunities, experiences or relationships this limiting identity has cost you. Be honest about what you've missed.

Time: 10 minutes

Day 5: Catch It Live

Today, just notice when your limiting identity is active. Don't try to change it, just catch it. Set 3 phone reminders to ask: "Is my limiting identity running the show right now?"

Time: 2 minutes, 3 times

Day 6: Design Your New Identity

Write your empowering alternative: "I am becoming someone who..." Make it believable but inspiring. Read it aloud 10 times.

The 30-Day Identity Wheel Transformation Plan

Time: 10 minutes

Day 7: Evidence Hunt

Find 3 pieces of evidence from your past that support your new identity, even small ones. Write them down.

Time: 15 minutes

Week 2: Stop the Old Pattern (Days 8–14)

"Between stimulus and response there is a space. In that space is our power to choose."

Day 8: The Pattern Interrupt

Every time you catch your limiting identity active today, say "Cancel, cancel" (out loud or mentally) and immediately state your new identity instead.

Time: Throughout day

Day 9: Question Everything

When limiting thoughts arise today, ask: "Is this thought absolutely true? How do I feel when I believe it? Who would I be without it?" (From Byron Katie's method mentioned in your book.)

Time: As needed

Day 10: Emotional Distancing

When you feel emotions from your old identity, practise saying: "I notice anxiety arising" instead of "I am anxious". Create space between you and the emotion.

Time: As needed

Day 11: Fear as Information

Identify one action your new identity would take that scares you. Don't take it yet, just write it down and notice: What is this fear trying to protect me from?

Time: 10 minutes

Day 12: Environment Audit

Remove or modify one environmental trigger that activates your limiting identity. This could be unfollowing someone on social media, changing your workspace or avoiding a specific situation.

Time: 20 minutes

Day 13: The 90-Second Rule

When strong emotions from your old identity arise, remember: the chemical cascade lasts 90 seconds. Set a timer and just observe the feeling without acting on it.

Time: As needed

Day 14: Power Pose Day

Three times today, when you feel your limiting identity active, stand in a power pose for 2 minutes (hands on hips, chest open, chin up). Notice how your internal state shifts.

Time: 6 minutes total

Week 3: Install the New Pattern (Days 15–21)

"We become what we practise most."

Day 15: First New Action

Take ONE action today that your new identity would take, even if it feels uncomfortable. Start small: make the phone call, speak up in the meeting, go for the walk.

Time: Varies

Day 16: Morning Identity Priming

Start your day by looking in the mirror and stating your new identity 3 times with conviction. Feel it in your body, not just your head.

Time: 5 minutes

Day 17: Visualisation Installation

Spend 10 minutes vividly imagining yourself fully embodying your new identity. See it, feel it, hear what others say about you. Make it real in your mind.

Time: 10 minutes

Day 18: Social Identity Test

Tell one trusted person about your new identity and ask them to notice when you embody it. Make it real by sharing it.

Time: 15 minutes

Day 19: Evidence Collection

Start an evidence journal. Write down 3 ways you acted from your new identity today, no matter how small.

Time: 10 minutes

Day 20: Identity-Aligned Goal

Set one specific goal that your new identity would naturally achieve in the next 30 days. Make it concrete and measurable.

Time: 15 minutes

Day 21: The Hard Conversation

Have one conversation you've been avoiding because your old identity said you couldn't handle it. Your new identity can.

Time: Varies

Week 4: Make It Stick (Days 22–30)

"Identity change is the ultimate level of change."

Day 22: Stress Test

The 30-Day Identity Wheel Transformation Plan

Intentionally maintain your new identity during a challenging situation today. This is where transformation becomes real.

Time: Varies

Day 23: Teach Someone Else

Explain your transformation process to someone else. Teaching solidifies your own change.

Time: 20 minutes

Day 24: Identity Expansion

Apply your new identity to a life area you haven't yet. If you're becoming "someone who takes care of their body" apply it to sleep, not just exercise.

Time: 10 minutes planning

Day 25: Future Self Dialogue Write a letter from your future self (1 year from now) who fully embodies this identity. What advice do they give you?

Time: 15 minutes

Day 26: Celebration Ritual

Acknowledge how far you've come. Compare yourself today to Day 1. Create a small celebration ritual for your transformation.

Time: 20 minutes

Day 27: Handle Doubters

Someone will question your change (maybe even you). Practise responding from your new identity rather than defending or proving.

Time: As needed

Day 28: Identity Integration

Spend today consciously operating from your new identity in ALL interactions: work, family, friends, strangers. Notice how it feels.

Time: Throughout day

Day 29: Create Your Power List

Design 5 daily actions that someone with your new identity would naturally do. This becomes your maintenance system.

Time: 15 minutes

Day 30: Next Evolution Planning

Your new identity is established. What's the next identity you want to develop? Plant the seed for your next 30-day transformation.

Time: 20 minutes

Completion Criteria

You've successfully transformed when:

✓ Your new identity feels natural (not forced) 70% of the time

✓ Others comment on positive changes they've noticed

The 30-Day Identity Wheel Transformation Plan

✓ You automatically think/act from new identity during challenges

✓ You can help someone else with similar identity transformation

✓ You've taken actions your old identity would never have taken

If you're not there yet: Repeat week 3-4 with the same identity before moving to a new one.

Maintenance: Continue your Power List daily + monthly identity check-ins.

Emergency Support

Stuck on any day?

- Do it badly rather than not at all
- Ask: "What would someone with my new identity do right now?"
- Remember: Progress, not perfection

Old identity returns strongly?

- It's a normal part of change, expect it
- Return to Day 8 pattern interrupt techniques
- Review your evidence journal from Day 19

Want to quit?

- Just do today's task, nothing else
- Remember why you started (Day 4)
- Contact your support person from Day 18

The Next Step in Your Transformation Journey

While this 30-Day Identity Wheel transformation plan provides a powerful framework for self-directed change, many people discover that deep identity transformation benefits tremendously from structured guidance and community support. Just as elite athletes work with coaches to reach their full potential, partnering with someone who understands the nuances of the Identity Wheel can accelerate your growth exponentially.

If you've found value in these concepts and want to experience a more immersive, guided approach to transformation, my Ascend coaching programme offers precisely that. Ascend builds upon the Identity Wheel framework with personalised support, advanced techniques and a community of like-minded people committed to their own evolution.

Your journey doesn't end with this book; in many ways, it's just beginning. Whether you continue applying these principles independently or choose to work with others, remember that transformation is not a destination but an ongoing process of becoming more authentically and powerfully yourself.

References

Chapter 1: The Wheel: Understanding the Cyclical Nature of Personal Growth

[1] Clark, A. (2013). Whatever next? Predictive brains, situated agents, and the future of cognitive science. *Behavioral and Brain Sciences, 36*(3), 181–204.

[2] Dweck, C. S. (2016). *Mindset: The new psychology of success* (Updated ed.). Ballantine Books.

[3] Feldman Barrett, L. (2017). *How emotions are made: The secret life of the brain.* Pan Macmillan.

[4] Hayes, S. C., Strosahl, K. D., & Wilson, K. G. (2016). *Acceptance and commitment therapy: The process and practice of mindful change* (2nd ed.). Guilford Press.

Chapter 2: The Mind's Hidden Architecture

[5] Arden, J. B. (2019). *Mind-brain-gene: Toward psychotherapy integration.* W.W. Norton & Company.

[6] Lipton, B. H. (2015). *The biology of belief: Unleashing the power of consciousness, matter and miracles* (10th anniversary ed.). Hay House.

[7] Hebb, D. O. (2002). *The organization of behavior: A neuropsychological theory.* Psychology Press. (Original work published 1949.)

[8] Dispenza, J. (2017). *Becoming supernatural: How common people are doing the uncommon*. Hay House.

Chapter 3: Identity – The Core of Your Reality

[9] McAdams, D. P., & McLean, K. C. (2013). Narrative identity. *Current Directions in Psychological Science, 22*(3), 233–238.

[10] Oyserman, D., Elmore, K., & Smith, G. (2012). Self, self-concept, and identity. In M. R. Leary & J. P. Tangney (Eds.), *Handbook of self and identity* (2nd ed., pp. 69-104). Guilford Press.

[11] Erikson, E. H., & Erikson, J. M. (1997). *The life cycle completed* (Extended version). W.W. Norton.

[12] Damasio, A. (2018). *The strange order of things: Life, feeling, and the making of cultures*. Pantheon Books.

[13] Maddux, J. E. (2009). Self-efficacy: The power of believing you can. In S. J. Lopez & C. R. Snyder (Eds.), *Oxford handbook of positive psychology* (2nd ed., pp. 335-343). Oxford University Press.

Chapter 4: The Power of Thoughts and Beliefs

[14] Beck, A. T., & Haigh, E. A. P. (2014). Advances in cognitive theory and therapy: The generic cognitive model. *Annual Review of Clinical Psychology, 10*, 1–24.

[15] Kahneman, D. (2011). *Thinking, fast and slow*. Penguin Books.

[16] Kini, P., Wong, J., McInnis, S., Gabana, N., & Brown, J. (2016). The effects of gratitude expression on neural activity. *NeuroImage, 128*, 1–10.

[17] Kiken, L. G., Garland, E. L., Bluth, K., Palsson, O. S., & Gaylord, S. A. (2015). From a state to a trait: Trajectories of state mindfulness in

meditation during intervention predict changes in trait mindfulness. *Personality and Individual Differences, 81*, 41–46.

[18] Barrett, L. F. (2020). *Seven and a half lessons about the brain*. Houghton Mifflin Harcourt.

[19] Davidson, R. J., & Begley, S. (2012). *The emotional life of your brain: How its unique patterns affect the way you think, feel, and live—and how you can change them*. Hudson Street Press.

[20] Dispenza, J. (2015). *You are the placebo: Making your mind matter*. Hay House.

[21] Wood, A. M., Froh, J. J., & Geraghty, A. W. (2010). Gratitude and well-being: A review and theoretical integration. *Clinical Psychology Review, 30*(7), 890–905.

[22] Frith, C. D., & Frith, U. (2012). Mechanisms of social cognition. *Annual Review of Psychology, 63*, 287–313.

Chapter 5: Mastering Your Emotional Landscape

[23] Gross, J. J. (2015). Emotion regulation: Current status and future prospects. *Psychological Inquiry, 26*(1), 1–26.

[24] Barrett, L. F., Lewis, M., & Haviland-Jones, J. M. (Eds.). (2018). *Handbook of emotions* (4th ed.). The Guilford Press.

[27] Taylor, J. B. (2009). *My stroke of insight: A brain scientist's personal journey*. Penguin Books.

[28] Brach, T. (2019). *Radical compassion: Learning to love yourself and your world with the practice of RAIN*. Viking.

[29] Van der Kolk, B. (2014). *The body keeps the score: Brain, mind, and body in the healing of trauma*. Viking.

References

[30] Cuddy, A. J. C., Schultz, S. J., & Fosse, N. E. (2018). P-curving a more comprehensive body of research on postural feedback reveals clear evidential value for power-posing effects: Reply to Simmons and Simonsohn. *Psychological Science, 29*(4), 656–666.

Chapter 6: Beyond Fear – Reclaiming Your Power

[31] LeDoux, J. E. (2015). *Anxious: Using the brain to understand and treat fear and anxiety.* Viking.

[32] Porges, S. W. (2011). *The polyvagal theory: Neurophysiological foundations of emotions, attachment, communication, and self-regulation.* W.W. Norton & Company.

[33] Brown, B. (2018). *Dare to lead: Brave work. Tough conversations. Whole hearts.* Random House.

[34] Harris, R. (2019). *ACT made simple: An easy-to-read primer on acceptance and commitment therapy* (2nd ed.). New Harbinger Publications.

[35] Gilbert, P., & Choden. (2013). *Mindful compassion: How the science of compassion can help you understand your emotions, live in the present, and connect deeply with others.* New Harbinger Publications.

[36] Carleton, R. N. (2016). Fear of the unknown: One fear to rule them all? *Journal of Anxiety Disorders, 41*, 5–21.

[37] Steel, P. (2007). The nature of procrastination: A meta-analytic and theoretical review of quintessential self-regulatory failure. *Psychological Bulletin, 133*(1), 65–94.

[38] Rozin, P., & Royzman, E. B. (2001). Negativity bias, negativity dominance, and contagion. *Personality and Social Psychology Review, 5*(4), 296–320.

[39] Siegel, D. J. (2018). *Aware: The science and practice of presence.* TarcherPerigee.

[40] Cuddy, A. (2015). *Presence: Bringing your boldest self to your biggest challenges.* Little, Brown Spark.

[41] Brooks, A. W. (2014). Get excited: Reappraising pre-performance anxiety as excitement. *Journal of Experimental Psychology: General, 143*(3), 1144–1158.

Chapter 7: Action – Bridging the Knowing-Doing Gap

[42] Pfeffer, J., & Sutton, R. I. (2000). *The knowing-doing gap: How smart companies turn knowledge into action.* Harvard Business School Press.

[43] Frisella, A. (2018). *75 Hard: A tactical guide to winning the war with yourself.* 44Seven Media.

[44] Duhigg, C. (2012). *The power of habit: Why we do what we do in life and business.* Random House.

[45] Clear, J. (2018). *Atomic habits: An easy & proven way to build good habits & break bad ones.* Random House Business.

[46] Fogg, B. J. (2019). *Tiny habits: The small changes that change everything.* Virgin Books.

[47] Pink, D. H. (2018). *When: The scientific secrets of perfect timing.* Canongate Books.

[48] Brown, B. (2015). *Rising strong: How the ability to reset transforms the way we live, love, parent, and lead.* Random House.

References

Chapter 8: Breaking the Confirmation Loop

[49] Seligman, M. E. P. (2018). *The hope circuit: A psychologist's journey from helplessness to optimism.* PublicAffairs.

[50] Tosi, J., & Warmke, B. (2016). Moral grandstanding. *Philosophy & Public Affairs, 44*(3), 197–217.

[51] McRaney, D. (2011). *You are not so smart: Why you have too many friends on Facebook, why your memory is mostly fiction, and 46 other ways you're deluding yourself.* Gotham Books.

Chapter 9: Transforming Your Reality Through Mindset

[52] Dweck, C. S. (2012). *Mindset: Changing the way you think to fulfil your potential.* Robinson.

[53] Oettingen, G. (2014). *Rethinking positive thinking: Inside the new science of motivation.* Current.

[54] Vohs, K. D., Redden, J. P., & Rahinel, R. (2013). Physical order produces healthy choices, generosity, and conventionality, whereas disorder produces creativity. *Psychological Science, 24*(9), 1860–1867.

[55] Knight, J. (2019). *The collaborative leader: The ultimate leadership challenge.* Robinson.

[56] Fowler, J. H., & Christakis, N. A. (2008). Dynamic spread of happiness in a large social network: longitudinal analysis over 20 years in the Framingham Heart Study. *British Medical Journal, 337*, a2338.

[57] Achor, S., & Gielan, M. (2015). Consuming negative news can make you less effective at work. *Harvard Business Review.*

[58] Gross, J. J. (2019). Emotion regulation: A valuation perspective. In A. S. Fox, R. C. Lapate, A. J. Shackman, & R. J. Davidson (Eds.), *The nature of*

emotion: Fundamental questions (2nd ed., pp. 453–456). Oxford University Press.

[59] Seligman, M. E. P. (2011). *Flourish: A visionary new understanding of happiness and well-being.* Free Press.

Chapter 10: Sustaining Your Transformation

[60] Norcross, J. C., & Vangarelli, D. J. (1988). The resolution solution: longitudinal examination of New Year's change attempts. *Journal of Substance Abuse, 1*(2), 127–134.

[61] Prigogine, I., & Stengers, I. (2018). *Order out of chaos: Man's new dialogue with nature.* Verso Books.

[62] McGonigal, K. (2012). *The willpower instinct: How self-control works, why it matters, and what you can do to get more of it.* Avery.

[63] Loehr, J., & Schwartz, T. (2003). *The power of full engagement: Managing energy, not time, is the key to high performance and personal renewal.* Free Press.

[64] Fredrickson, B. L. (2009). *Positivity: Groundbreaking research reveals how to embrace the hidden strength of positive emotions, overcome negativity, and thrive.* Crown.

[65] Jha, A. P., Morrison, A. B., Dainer-Best, J., Parker, S., Rostrup, N., & Stanley, E. A. (2015). Minds "at attention": Mindfulness training curbs attentional lapses in military cohorts. *PLOS ONE, 10*(2), e0116889.

[66] Grant, H., & Schwartz, B. (2011). Too much of a good thing: The challenge and opportunity of the inverted U. Perspectives on Psychological Science, 6(1), 61-76.

[67] Lazar, S. W., Kerr, C. E., Wasserman, R. H., Gray, J. R., Greve, D. N., Treadway, M. T., McGarvey, M., Quinn, B. T., Dusek, J. A., Benson, H., Rauch,

References

S. L., Moore, C. I., & Fischl, B. (2005). Meditation experience is associated with increased cortical thickness. *Neuroreport, 16*(17), 1893-1897.

[68] Davidson, R. J., Kabat-Zinn, J., Schumacher, J., Rosenkranz, M., Muller, D., Santorelli, S. F., Urbanowski, F., Harrington, A., Bonus, K., & Sheridan, J. F. (2003). Alterations in brain and immune function produced by mindfulness meditation. *Psychosomatic Medicine, 65*(4), 564-570.

[69] Brewer, J. A., Worhunsky, P. D., Gray, J. R., Tang, Y. Y., Weber, J., & Kober, H. (2011). Meditation experience is associated with differences in default mode network activity and connectivity. *Proceedings of the National Academy of Sciences, 108*(50), 20254-20259.

[70] Kosslyn, S. M., Ganis, G., & Thompson, W. L. (2001). Neural foundations of imagery. *Nature Reviews Neuroscience, 2*(9), 635-642.

[71] Richardson, A. (1967). Mental practice: A review and discussion part I. *Research Quarterly. American Association for Health, Physical Education and Recreation, 38*(1), 95-107.

[72] Newberg, A., & Waldman, M. R. (2009). *How God Changes Your Brain: Breakthrough Findings from a Leading Neuroscientist*. Ballantine Books.

[73] Garfield, C. A., & Bennett, H. Z. (1984). *Peak Performance: Mental Training Techniques of the World's Greatest Athletes*. Warner Books

[74] Maltz, M. (1960). *Psycho-Cybernetics: A New Way to Get More Living Out of Life*. Prentice-Hall.

[75] Pascual-Leone, A. (2001). The plastic human brain cortex. *Annual Review of Neuroscience, 24*, 185-208.

[76] Ayres, J., & Hopf, T. (1992). Visualization: reducing speech anxiety and enhancing performance. *Communication Reports, 5*(1), 1-10.

[77] McNorgan, C. (2012). Frontiers in Human Neuroscience, 6, 285.

[78] Damasio, A. R. (1994). Descartes' Error: Emotion, Reason, and the Human Brain.

[79] Slater, M., et al. (2010). PLoS One, 5(5), e10564.

[80] Holmes, P. S., & Collins, D. J. (2001). Journal of Applied Sport Psychology, 13(1), 60-83.

[81] Klimesch, W. (2012). Alpha-band oscillations, attention, and controlled access to stored information. *Trends in Cognitive Sciences*, 16(12), 606-617.

Chapter 11: The Identity Wheel in Practice

[82] Gottman, J. M., & Silver, N. (2015). *The seven principles for making marriage work: A practical guide from the country's foremost relationship expert.* Harmony.

[83] Kozhevnikov, M., Evans, C., & Kosslyn, S. M. (2014). Cognitive style as environmentally sensitive individual differences in cognition: A modern synthesis and applications in education, business, and management. *Psychological Science in the Public Interest*, 15(1), 3-33.

[84] Mann, T., Tomiyama, A. J., Westling, E., Lew, A. M., Samuels, B., & Chatman, J. (2007). Medicare's search for effective obesity treatments: Diets are not the answer. *American Psychologist*, 62(3), 220-233.

[85] Christakis, N. A., & Fowler, J. H. (2013). Social contagion theory: Examining dynamic social networks and human behavior. *Statistics in Medicine*, 32(4), 556-577.

[86] Oura, R., & Shimada, S. (2019). Personality change predicts changes in brain activity, particularly in reward processing. *NeuroImage*, 184, 795-803.

Acknowledgements

To Gavin Hinchliffe for giving me the kick I needed to finally get this book written.

To Hayley Williams for your meticulous proofreading work.

To Paul James, Steven James, Louisa Holman and Elizabeth Green for reading the initial drafts and providing invaluable feedback.

To Katie Keward for your unwavering belief in me.

To Theodore Wolf for being a legend.

To Mollie, Sean, Kelly and Andy for courageously sharing your transformation stories in such detail.

To everyone who supported this project in ways both seen and unseen - my heartfelt gratitude.

And to Leremy Gan for the Stick Figures Artwork. (www.leremy.com)

www.ingramcontent.com/pod-product-compliance
Lightning Source LLC
Chambersburg PA
CBHW052209090526
44584CB00016BA/1740